Misa, Mesa
y Musa

Liturgy in the
U.S. Hispanic Church

second edition

Misa, Mesa y Musa

Liturgy in the U.S. Hispanic Church

Compiled and Edited by
Kenneth G. Davis, OFM, CONV.

WORLD LIBRARY PUBLICATIONS
a division of J. S. Paluch Co., Inc.
3825 N. Willow Road, Schiller Park, Illinois, 60176

Kenneth G. Davis, Compiler and Editor

Misa, Mesa y Musa: Liturgy in the U.S. Hispanic Church
Second Edition
Copyright © 1997, WORLD LIBRARY PUBLICATIONS,
a division of J.S. Paluch Company
3825 North Willow Road
Schiller Park, IL 60176
All rights reserved.

Produced in assication with
Instituto de Liturgia Hispana
P.O. Box 29387
Washington, D.C. 20017-0387

Publication of this book was made possible in part by
a generous grant from the ACTA foundation, Chicago.

Cover: *La Conquistadora de Tepeyac*
Copyright © 1991, G. E. Mullan, Rainbird Graphics,
San Antonio, Texas
Used with permission.

Alan J. Hommerding, Production Editor

Cover design by Elizabeth Rizo

Body layout and design by Alan J. Hommerding

Maggie Redmond, Typesetter

CONTENTS

ACKNOWLEDGMENTS

I would like to thank Daniel McGuire of the J. S. Paluch Company for his initial support of this project. Also I am grateful to the board of directors of the *Instituto de Liturgia Hispana* for their early and unwavering support. Alan Hommerding brought the project to its conclusion as production editor.

In the selection process I was ably assisted by the librarians of the Oblate School of Theology: Clifford Dawdy, María Garcia, Eugene Sanders, and Rosemary Butler.

Of course, all the contributors deserve a debt of thanks. Some of their work was previously published. Their publishers were kind enough to allow us to reprint those articles here. Therefore I thank and acknowledge: 1) The Liturgical Press for Timothy M. Matovina's article "Ministries and the Servant Community," which appeared in *Worship*, and for the article by Arturo J. Pérez, "Signs of the Times: Towards a Hispanic Rite, *Quizas*," which appeared in volume 3, number 4 of *New Theology Review* (November, 1990); 2) Alan Hommerding, editor of *AIM* in which appeared my article and those of my colleagues at the Oblate School of Theology; 3) the publishers of *Liturgical Ministry* which originally printed the article of Mary Frances Reza, "Crosscultural Music Making," volume 3 (Fall, 1994).

The title of this book comes to me from Rosa María Icaza who, in turn, received it from Rev. Ovidio Pecharromán, OP. I dedicate the book to her and all the other pioneers of the *Instituto de Liturgia Hispana*. ¡Que vivan!

CONTRIBUTORS

Kenneth G. Davis, O.F.M., Conv. is director of the Doctor of Ministry Program at the Oblate School of Theology in San Antonio.

Dr. Lorenzo R. Florián is an international speaker, author, and composer. He resides in Chicago.

Raúl Gómez, SDS is a presbyter of the Society of the Divine Savior.

Ms. Sally Gómez-Kelley, MTS directs the supervised ministry program at the Oblate School of Theology in San Antonio, TX.

Paulina Hurtado, O.P. is a candidate for the Doctor of Ministry degree at the Catholic University of America.

Rosa María Icaza, C.C.V.I., Ph.D. is the Director of the Pastoral Department at the Mexican American Cultural Center in San Antonio, TX.

Padre Jaime Lara, Ph.D. is adjunct professor of Liturgy at Yale University Divinity School, New Haven, CT.

Reverend Jóse López teaches preaching and pastoral care at the Oblate School of Theology in San Antonio, TX.

Timothy Matovina, Ph.D. is assistant professor of theology at Loyola Marymount University in Los Angeles.

Arturo Pérez Rodríguez is a priest of the Archdiocese of Chicago, lecturer, and writer on Hispanic Liturgy and Spirituality.

Bishop Ricardo Ramírez is the ordinary bishop of the diocese of Las Cruces, NM.

Mary Frances Reza works for the Albuquerque Public Schools. She is the author of two books, and has extensive experience in music and worship.

Ms. Sylvia Sánchez is the vice-president of the National Catholic Council on Hispanic Ministry.

Reverend Juan Sosa is Executive Director of the Ministry of Worship and Spiritual Life for the Archdiocese of Miami, and pastor of St. Catherine of Sienna Catholic Church in Kendall, FL.

Doris Turek, SSND is an attorney-at-law, and executive director of the Instituto de Liturgia Hispana.

INTRODUCTION

I am not a wine connoisseur. Being from Kentucky, bourbon is more my drink. Therefore, on those rare occasions when I dine at a restaurant with a wine list, I rely on a knowledgeable server to guide my selection.

This introduction is written especially to help those unfamiliar with Hispanic liturgy to savor the contents of this book, and to select those aspects most conducive to making the Mass a meal of welcome and wonder. Like a good server, I will explain what is available, and help your selection. One difference between myself and the server is that, as editor, I will be explaining a list that I selected myself. Of course, the entire book is worth reading and saving for future reference.

All the selections have common elements. First, they are readable. Second, each chapter is an example of praxis, i.e., research and meditation on experience reflected back to the agents of that experience for their pastoral use and further contemplation. Nearly all the authors deal with personal experience, offer practical applications, and evidence the integration of careful research in the service of pastoral care. Therefore, not only the content but the methodology were important criteria for selection. Third, this distilled wisdom represents some of the best vintage available. While a few of these essays were previously published, they are often difficult to find. Some are from conferences which were never recorded or are otherwise inaccessible. They have all aged well, and are for the first time easily available to scholar and pastor alike. While each is distinct, they are mutually complementary.

Bishop Ricardo Ramírez begins in a very particular context, the local parish. This is where the thing we call liturgy happens. His is a robust, explicit exposition. He deals frankly with the issue of leadership (not only "white, masculine, educated, economically advantaged or adult"). While Jaime Lara gives an historical defense of popular religion, the Bishop uses a compelling story from his youth to argue a similar point. Mary Frances Reza provides a scholarly exposition of liturgical music; Ramírez simply calls for music that is not pacific but prophetic. Rosa María Icaza explores at length one issue Bishop Ramírez raises: "Do We Have Inculturated Liturgies?" She gives no simplistic answers. An earthy tone of practical example finishes her brief exploration of liturgy and inculturation. While willing to confront various aspects of her own culture which resist the Gospel, Sister Icaza excels in displaying those cultural resources which do resonate with liturgical excellence.

Popular religion often preserved these resources. Jaime Lara gives perhaps the best general historical and liturgical defense of this most ancient U.S. Catholic spirituality ever attempted. Not only does he touch upon some half-dozen examples, he suggests that "… an Hispanic liturgical innovation for the 'heathens' in the New World became the liturgical practice of the Universal Church!" This bubbly chapter is well worth savoring.

Jóse López offers an excellent example of the methodology mentioned above. He looks at Hispanic popular religion in relation to our liturgical calendar. Respecting both, he shows how they can enrich each other. López is a scholar and a pastor who presents no contrasts between the two; there is a well-rounded aftertaste to this flavorful blend.

The previous authors all deal with the largest U.S. Hispanic group, those of Mexican descent. It is important to understand that there is as much difference between various Latino/a groups as there is between French and Californian wines. We must note their similarity but also their particularity.

To that end, Juan Sosa offers a wonderful fusion of flavors with his history and contemporary pastoral recommendations concerning two saints popular with Cubans: *Santa Barbara* and *San Lorenzo*. Like Raúl Gómez, Sosa appreciates the strength of Hispanic women, who are sometimes supposed to be only oppressed. Saint Barbara not only endured torture and death, she became the patron of a decidedly daring group—artillery men. What Reza does with music, Sosa does briefly with visual art. He shows how African slaves reinterpreted the imagery of these saints and thereby included them in the pantheon of *Santería*. Incidentally, Santa Barbara becomes transmuted as Chango, god of war and thunder. Hardly a demure deity!

The syncretism Sosa uncorks is a fermenting issue. Perhaps his greatest insight is how this blending, which resulted from barbarity, testifies to the unquenchable thirst of the religious intuition which strives, even under slavery, to bridge "racial differences and social distinctions."

Puertorriqueña Sally Gómez Kelley lives and gives a fine example of what may be termed Hispanics' congenital multiculturalism. By that I do not mean the cheap opinion that culture is like a *serape*, a garment easily donned or discarded. Rather, I mean the realization that Latina/os, while particular, are also uniquely universal. The Arabs conquered Spain and mixed with the previous population. Their descendants mixed culturally and biologically with the indigenous peoples of America and Africa. Later, Asian and Europeans migrated and added to the mix. Gómez Kelley explores how she became more Puerto Rican by respecting both the differences and similarities between herself and other members of what José Vasconcelos calls the "cosmic race."

Ramírez and Icaza ably introduce liturgy and inculturation. Sosa and Gómez-Kelley explore peculiar examples of these phenomena. This is the soil and the sun that brought forth these varied vintages. But who brings the grape from the arbor to the bottle? Ministers are charged to harvest with care, process with patience, and oversee the slow fermentation of these ingredients. Ministry is the topic of the chapters by Arturo Pérez and Timothy Matovina.

At first I thought naïve Pérez's assertion that *los viejos* (the elderly) never lie. But revisiting his essay helped me explore this metaphor more. Quite simply: there is a wisdom to survival. Those who live longer than a good bottle of wine are, by their very example, nonfiction books of wisdom. They are the embodiments of the earliest U.S. Christian spirituality: Latino/a popular religion. It is their sense of the ascetic and aesthetic which brings ardor to our order and reverence to our rituals. The lie lies not in the ancient intuition found in this popular religion. Perhaps the falsehood is the youthful confidence that the divine can best be experienced through the practiced programs of spare ceremonies. Maybe we have moveable feasts to remind us that we cannot stay the Spirit.

Matovina shares this respect for people's religious practices, and the role of ministers who must use those rites as a resource for liturgy. He not only deals with these formal and informal rituals, but with official and nonofficial liturgical leadership. Please note that his suggestion to renew the marriage rite has in fact been implemented by the Episcopal Conference of Spain. Matovina may not be read in Spain, but he was accurately reading the needs of the people.

Of the ministries that seek to explore the resource of religion in home and connect it with the liturgy in Church, music and presiding have paramount importance. My own essay deals with one presider stretching to touch the two. It is a pleasure to present another approach.

What would liturgy be without music? And what would Hispanic liturgical music be without Mary Frances Reza? Her contribution is rich and varied. It goes well with almost anything. She touches upon historical points worthy of future research. She is both ecumenical in breadth and personal in tone. This exploration of the problem and promise of respecting at once an austere Roman rite and a baroque, Hispanic intuition is fascinating. It is worth sniffing, sipping, and savoring its suggestive qualities. Compare this with the unique new taste of the music and writing of Lorenzo Florián; his work is a fine example of the second generation of U.S. Hispanic liturgical musicians for whom Reza prepared the way.

I confess to being at a kind of *mestizo* moment in life. I am young enough to continue to be convinced of the importance of youth, especially among Latino/as who are so much younger than we Euro-Americans. Yet I am old enough to get quickly exhausted by their inexhaustible, effervescent energy.

One simply cannot do Hispanic ministry without doing youth ministry. The demographics are clear. Liturgically, one of the most important moments in which to celebrate youth is the *quinceañera*. It is with pride that we save this clear, fruity draught for last. No sediment here; in fact, no sentimentality. Raúl Gómez not only deals with the history and theology of the rite, but shows its inherent vitality, and its import especially to young women. Although I suspect it is more modern (dating from the Emperor Maximilian) than Gómez suggests, undoubtedly it is of contemporary urgency. While his chapter deals with a group too young to drink wine, it is an age group pivotal to the life of the Church. Taste and see.

For those interested in researching a particular topic or author, we provide a select bibliography. Readers who are not bilingual will be glad to note that there is also a glossary of Spanish terms.

This is our wine list, a heady mixture of complementary delights. They have been selected with care and are presented with pride.

Misa (Mass) and *Mesa* (Table/Meal) are obvious places for choice wine. More than one poet has found the *Musa* (Muse) enticed to tarry by a good glass. We offer these varied wines to scholars and pastors, musicians and poets, preachers and researchers.

¡Salud!

Kenneth G. Davis, O.F.M., Conv.

Weaving the Tapestry: the Task of the Church in the U.S.

Bishop Ricardo Ramírez

How might we better invite the different cultures of our multi-cultured Church to come, share their stories, their talents and spirituality, to be part of the enterprise that began almost 2,000 years ago?

Like Joseph in the Old Testament who had a technicolor dreamcoat, the Church in the United States is also of many colors. This multi-hued coat of the Church has been getting more colorful over the years. It is most beautiful, this coat that God willed our particular Church to have.

Some countries have a geographical place: a Canterbury, a Lourdes, a Guadalupe, a Fatima, a martyr's shrine, a Compostela, a Jerusalem or a Rome as symbols that characterize their spiritual heritage and tell their story of faith. Our heritage is our dreamcoat, the composite makeup of a Church. It is many-hued: black, brown, white, with our pluriform European background, our Native and Latin American Indigenous roots, and our Asian connections, our most recent gifts.

Dr. Vasconcelos, an eminent educator from Mexico, used to get sentimental about the Mexican race and say that it was a "cosmic" race. That is because it brought together the Asian, the European, and the Native-American to form the new *mestizo* people of Mexico. I would suggest that we, the Catholic Church in the United States, might be the "cosmic church." We too are characterized by not one particular racial or national genre, but by just about as many peoples as make up the world. It is in countries such as the U.S. which have seen great immigration that we see the Catholicity or the universalism of the Church.

But it is not just the racial and national characteristics that form the gift that is our U.S. Church. Rather it is precisely the spiritual heritage of faith that all these groups bring to the whole. This is where the gift lies, in the hearts of the believing people who come to live with us. The various peoples bring with them precious jars and barrels, boxes and trunks, baskets and pots, sacks and bags...all full of God's bounty; a victorious faith won by heroic and courageous women and men who sustained their belief in Jesus and the Church against horrible odds. Every national group has a story to tell of persecution and martyrdom, of prejudice and oppression: if each group represented in our Church placed

7

before the others their faith-storybooks, what an array of books we would have.

First is the dramatic contribution of the Native-American peoples with their tremendous wealth of spiritual wisdom. Then there is the centuries-old presence of the Hispanic peoples, and the courageous stories of the African-American and Cajun-Catholics. Imagine the stories of faith of the Catholics from England, Ireland, Scotland, Spain, Portugal, Germany, Holland, Belgium, France, Italy, and the eastern European countries such as Poland, Czechoslovakia, Lithuania, and Croatia. The stories of faith of the Filipino, the Japanese, the Vietnamese, the Chinese and Indian Catholics, and the others of the Far East—each in their own way— are able to provide us with dramatic recitations of their own salvation history.

However, we can only begin to address the possible practical solutions of being an inviting Church after we have considered other basic questions: 1) To what are we going to invite others to join? 2) Are we ready to invite? 3) Are we really doing what we are supposed to do as Church? In other words, do we have something to offer newcomers, and will they really be better off with us? Will we be open to their possible contributions to our Church life?

THE "HEY, LOOK AT US" ISSUES

Evangelii Nuntiandi reminds us that evangelization and welcoming go hand in hand. Pope Paul VI made the emphatic challenge that the Church really portray itself as community. I am sure he had the parish in mind when he said that a community will know that it is evangelizing when the people around it ask such questions as: "Why are they the way they are? Why do they love each other the way they do? Why are they for us?" These questions are automatically provoked by a true and authentic community.

What finally convinced St. Augustine that he should join the Church was the singing of the Alleluias. Probably those people were truly expressing their love of one another and were singing joyfully in unison because they were present to one another.

The Church as community happens existentially at the parish level. It is there that people share, participate, know one another, and exercise the virtues of compassion and charity.

The Church does not really happen at the universal level nor even at the diocesan level; it happens at the local level of the parish.

Gary Bradley says in *The Parish: Sacrament of Presence* (Franciscan Communications, Los Angeles, CA, 1982) that parish means:

> Christ's presence among people. Parish means a set of persons, a community in which and with which Jesus Christ reconfirms the presence of God. It is through the parish that we are directed towards the good in order to lead lives really worthy of human beings.

It is the community that creates liturgy. But it goes the other way around as well. A good liturgy can remind us of our commonality and our call to contribute to the common good.

A good liturgy reminds us of the call to exercise social justice in the world. Coming to the one table to eat of the one Bread, drink of the same Cup, and repeat the same Our Father has to remind us of justice. I quote from Bob Hovda ("The Mass and Its Social Consequences," *Liturgy '90*. April 1991):

> Where else in our society are all of us—not just a gnostic elite, but everyone—called to be social critics, called to extricate ourselves from the powers and principalities that claim to rule our daily lives, in order to submit ourselves to the sole dominion of God before whom all of us are equal? Where else in our society are we all addressed and sprinkled and bowed to and incensed and touched and kissed and treated like somebody—all in the very same way? Where else do economic czars and beggars get the same treatment? Where else are food and drink blessed in a common prayer of thanksgiving, broken and poured out, so that everybody, everybody shares and shares alike?

Let me add to what Bob Hovda says and go beyond his words. Our earthly liturgies point to the dream of the Kingdom of Jesus. The Kingdom points to equality, freedom, and the dignity of everyone. The Kingdom calls for sharing, compassion, and people looking after people, and people looking after those who might otherwise be excluded. In the liturgy, we exercise brotherhood and sisterhood in a preeminent way. It is true; we are all equal when we come to worship and to eat at the one table. All of this points to the ideal that, before God, all are the same and all should benefit from the goods of the Earth and no one should take advantage of anyone else. This is eminently implicit in the words of the Our Father. If God is the Father of all, we can exclude no one from His table or from the harvest of the Earth. No one should go hungry, no one should be illtreated, and no one should take advantage of anyone else. In the dream of God's Kingdom there is no room for exclusivism, elitism, sexism, nor racism.

Should not the consultative bodies in our parishes be expressive of all this? Should not what we say in liturgy be expressed in our parish life? None of our consultative bodies or leadership groups should be exclusive in the sense that they are only white, masculine, educated, economically advantaged, or adult.

Our Catholic people in the United States are among the most generous in the world. I have lived in four different countries and travelled to many more, and I have never seen so many service organizations nor so many charitable causes. We give millions of dollars each year to charity. Unfortunately, our people, including Catholics, sometimes do not want to see beyond their charitable responsibilities. Many feel that by simply donating to this or that cause their conscience can be at rest. But it is also important that we look to the root causes of poverty, hunger, and homelessness. I am disappointed, for example, that so many of our Catholic people strongly disagree with the work funded by the Campaign for Human Development, and in particular, the work of community organizing. So many of our people get very nervous when the poor and the powerless begin to empower themselves.

If the Church in the U.S. is to be truly welcoming to all peoples, then it must be true to its social mission in the world, and true to the radical demands of the Gospel. It is unfortunate that, in so many of our Churches, we have "tamed" the Eucharist and the Scriptures. By this I mean that the Christian message is often watered down and we seem to echo the gentle message of fundamentalism: "Jesus loves you just as you are." While it is true that Jesus loves us just as we are, it is also true that Christ demands hard things of us.

A great amount of our liturgical music, for example, pacifies rather than challenges us. When I go to Latin America I cannot help but notice the radical difference in the songs they sing. Their songs are of liberation, justice, equality, and hope. Ours are gentle and soothing. While there has to be a certain amount of comfort in our liturgy, it cannot be only that; liturgy must not create congregations that are apathetic and indifferent to the world.

THE "GETTING ALONG" ISSUES

The welcoming Church has to be more than just the society that surrounds it. Pastoralists speak of the Church's challenge to be counter-cultural. We have a prophetic mission, and sometimes we have to be different from others if we want to be true to this mission. Our Church cannot exclude the poor, those who are different (the second- and third-hand car families), the divorced, the separated, the unmarried mothers and their children or alienated youth.

We need a massive educational effort of the people in our churches. I am speaking of an education toward acceptance and getting along. The only way we can begin to solve some of these problems is if we begin to speak with one another and learn from one another's experiences.

In so many of our parishes our white Catholics have never had a conversation with a black person. In Las Cruces, NM we had the funeral of a beautiful Hispanic woman. She was so gracious, good, and generous in sharing her talents with all people. It was through her generosity to everyone that people got to know of the virtues of the Hispanic woman. Had it not been for her, many people would perhaps have gone through life full of biases against those with whom they were never given a chance to become familiar.

Perhaps what we need are inter-parish or bi-parish programs where we can create racial, cultural, and economic mixes. Perhaps "twining" is the answer, but not just at the level of financial assistance but at the level of real interchange and dialogue. For instance, I often visit prisons and jails and listen to the frustrations of our ministers who work there. Their frustrations stem from the fact that after the inmates are freed, there is no one to continue to minister to them in the outside world. We could connect and coordinate the work of our prison and jail ministries to those of our parishes.

THE "HOWDY DO" ISSUES

At all costs, we have to learn how to avoid turning people away. It saddens me when some of our people (for reasons of their own) turn to Protestant sects. However, I am extremely angry when we ourselves, the Catholic Church, run people out and almost encourage them to leave us by our treatment of them. I think that there are certain practices in our Church that are less than welcoming. This was the point of Bishop John McCarthy's November 1, 1992 letter to the priests, deacons, lay ministers, and parish support staffs of the Austin Diocese: "On Refusing Sacraments to 'Nominal' Catholics." I concur most emphatically with his statement:

> Other parishes have created procedures which—while in accord with the letter of the law—are so rigid and so demanding that people seeking the sacraments often go away discouraged because they believe they cannot meet the requirements.

It is unfortunate that some of our parish guidelines go beyond liturgical law and create obstacles to people of good faith who come to us seeking the sacraments.

People have to be prepared for the sacraments. We can have Christian commitment without ritual, but we must not tolerate ritual without Christian commitment. There have to be such things as educational and formational programs in preparation for sacraments. Yet sometimes these are presented as legalistic obstacles to be overcome rather than as aids toward a mutually desired goal.

I remember as a young priest observing people going from church to church trying to get a Baptism. They were told that they had to go for instruction. I worked with an older priest who was very kind, yet understanding of the need for sacramental preparation. When they had made the rounds and finally came to this priest, he would tell them, "Wow, you have come to the right place. We have just the thing for you. We've got a program that you would not believe. It will bring so much joy and peace to your life. I can hardly wait to get you into this program." The people would go away happy. Although they heard the very same thing from him that they heard from the other parishes, this priest presented it as an invitation rather than as a demand. So much depends on how we tell people about requirements. If rules are presented simply as rules, of course, that is going to scare people off. Furthermore, if we make fulfilling rules the most important criteria, then we are missing the boat.

If we are going to insist on preparation for sacraments, we must be certain of its quality. We cannot insist on classes, and then offer something that is mediocre. We had better make sure that what we are requiring is going to be good, substantial, and presented as an invitation and an opportunity to know Christ.

Remember, some new immigrants come from places where the rules are not as strict. It is not really their fault that they do not understand or appreciate our fascination with policies and rules. We should be happy they come to the rectory or office, and regard the situation as an opportunity to evangelize rather than as an occasion to scold or frighten.

We are being less than inviting at weddings and funerals, for example, if we react negatively when most of the congregation is obviously only nominally familiar with the sacraments. Again, these are occasions to evangelize rather than scoff. We priests are tempted on Ash Wednesday to berate people because they only come once a year and only to receive ashes. I have learned over the years to smile during Ash Wednesday even if my smile may not reflect what I really think or feel. We have to recognize our emotions but put on our best face and invite people back. If we show anger on those occasions then people will only feel that Church leadership is dysfunctional or irritable.

Our Church is increasingly Hispanic. The Hispanic cultures bring us a rich, popular religion that has a legitimacy all its own. It may not rate theologically as official worship or liturgy, but popular religion has been the nutrient of millions of people over the centuries, and for many, it has been their only recourse to God. Popular religion is different from superstition, fetishism, spiritism, or animism. Popular religion needs to be connected, reaffirmed, legitimized, and welcomed by our liturgical practices. As Mark Francis, CSV says in "Hispanic Popular Piety and Liturgical Reform," (*Modern Liturgy*, October 1991):

> Parish pastoral/liturgical outreach, ought to concentrate on how to support and enrich the practices of popular religiosity in the home by helping to imbue already traditional devotions with a rootedness

in the Scriptures and in the signs and symbols of the liturgical tradition of the Church which they often lack. Rather than ignoring or ridiculing these practices, a positive but critical evaluation of them by the church's 'religious professionals' would go a long way in healing the centuries-old gulf which separates them from the 'official liturgy.'

I am happy to see that many in the Church have finally legitimated the devotion to Our Lady of Guadalupe. It was just a few years ago that December 12 became an official celebration in the U.S. Church. Now it is common to see novenas, triduums, *mañanitas*, processions, and fiestas in honor of Our Lady of Guadalupe.

The pilgrimage, or *peregrinación*, is another very significant moment in the lives of Hispanic Christians. Perhaps we should help people prepare for pilgrimages, give them prayer services to conduct as they go, and welcome them back to the parish upon their return. During a liturgy we could possibly even have them relate their experiences.

THE "WE'RE GLAD YOU CAME" ISSUES

There is a place in our Church for bilingual and multilingual liturgies. There are times during the year that lend themselves to these kinds of multilingual and multi-cultural celebrations. May I suggest that the feasts of Christmas, Epiphany, Easter, Pentecost, the Fourth of July, and Thanksgiving are moments when we can liturgically celebrate the richness of our pluralistic society and Church. The Fourth of July is a good time to celebrate the arrival of new immigrants or the achievement of citizenship by parishioners. There is nothing wrong with having multilingual liturgies. In the U.S., even before Vatican II, we had masses in Latin, English, Greek, and Hebrew. No one is going to tell me that using various languages in the liturgy is something invented by modern-day liturgical crazies. It will be a welcoming gesture to different peoples if our bulletins, diocesan newspapers, and religious education materials appear in more than one language too.

The welcoming process is not just for the people initially approaching the Church. It lasts a lifetime. We need to follow up with those who enter the Church. The welcome does not stop when people are received. Remember the message of the Little Prince, "We are responsible for the rose we tame."

We have to invite the newly-arrived to share the richness of their spirituality and their journey of faith with others in ministry. We need to treat those who are coming in as adults, and not as children who need to be spoon-fed. For example, Hispanic religiosity deserves more than a patronizing pat on the head. It is a real, serious spirituality that has something to offer. Unfortunately, we are often biased against people who have an accent different from our own or who make grammatical mistakes. If people cannot speak our language we sometimes stop listening, and think that because they do not speak the way we do they have nothing to say. The Hispanic or any other cultural presence (Vietnamese, Irish, German, French) has a faith history that can enrich us all. Their message has to come to the heart of our parish life as part of our common treasure box. All people feel that they are part of something only when they contribute. The acceptance of their contribution offers meaning and importance to both the giver and the receiver.

Our parishes and diocesan chanceries, pastoral centers, schools, universities, and missions need to establish personnel policies that will reflect the multi-cultural richness of our Church. If "affirmative action" is a bad phrase, then perhaps "multi-cultural enrichment" is something to aim at.

CONCLUSION

I conclude with a story that I heard recently from Fr. Edmundo Rodríguez, S.J. Once upon a time, there was a couple window-shopping at a mall. They noticed an unusual sight, a man with long hair, a beard, wearing a long white robe. One told the other, "Is that who I think it is?" They approached the store, and sure enough, the sign said, "The Jesus Store." They went inside and asked the man, "Are you the person we think you are?"

"Yes, I am the Lord Jesus." Jesus asked them if they wanted to buy anything, and they said they'd look around. It was one of those stores where one fills out a form to designate the items to purchase. The items around the store were labeled, "Peace," "Justice," "A Drug-free Society," "No Poverty," "No Domestic Violence," "No Unemployment." The couple chose a few things such as "Peace" and "No Homelessness." They brought their completed form to Jesus and asked Him how much it was. He said, "You have made some very good choices!" But He told them that those items were very expensive. He gave them seeds, and He said, "You go out and plant these seeds, take care of these seedlings, water them, and nurture the plants. The fact is, however, you will not see the results during your lifetime, even though you might work very hard at bringing these things to fulfillment." The couple got very discouraged and went away without the seeds.

The Church is a favorite customer of "The Jesus Store." All of us have purchased some seeds, and they help us create a new Garden, the Kingdom of God. May God bless us all in our planting and nurturing of the seeds of justice, peace, and love.

Do We Have Inculturated Liturgies?

Rosa María Icaza, CCVI

Vatican II called for full and meaningful participation in liturgy. What cultural characteristics among Hispanics help or hinder their participation in liturgical celebrations? If we speak of an inculturated liturgy, we need to know first what we understand by liturgy and by culture. In *The Roman Liturgy and Inculturation*, John Paul II stated:

> To prepare an inculturation of the liturgy, Episcopal Conferences should call upon people who are competent both in the liturgical tradition of the Roman rite and in the appreciation of local cultural values...The liturgy... is at once the action of Christ the priest and the action of the Church which is his body...glorifying God and sanctifying humankind, achieved through visible signs. (21)

Liturgy is the praise of the Father by the total Christ, Head and members, in the power of the Spirit. Liturgy is the celebration (commemoration) of the Paschal Mystery: Life, passion, death, and resurrection of Christ. This mystery continues to be lived in our life as St. Paul tells us: "I rejoice in my sufferings for your sake, and in my flesh I am filling up what is lacking in the afflictions of Christ on behalf of his body, which is the Church" (Col 1:24). In the liturgy, therefore, we celebrate what we have lived, and then we live what we have celebrated.

The essential characteristics of liturgy are: 1) Communitarian communication with God [the Assembly is called together by God]; 2) Instruction through the Word of God, with the active, meaningful [conscious] and full participation of the faithful. Every liturgical celebration needs different ministers, and rites [ways of doing it] which are simple, brief, clear and without repetition. The Episcopal Conference [in some cases the local ordinary] and the Holy See must approve the rites.

If this is what we mean by liturgy, what do we mean by culture? Culture is a particular way of seeing and relating to God, others, and things. It is part of our entire life, i.e., philosophy, meaning, behavior, customs, values, symbols, etc. We learn our culture at home and through the environment in which we live.

Let us now take an historical look at some of the values of Hispanic peoples, particularly of the Mexican Americans. From the indigenous root (Prehistoric-1521), we have inherited a sense of community, religion incarnated in life, love for symbols, celebration of life and respect for our ancestors, living and dead. Because of our Iberian root (Prehistoric-1810), we are inclined to hospitality, to keeping the family together, to being loyal and faithful to one's own. Our Mexican ancestors (1810–1848) left us a deep Christian faith, love of Mary, hope in the midst of suffering, and concrete expressions of faith. From the United States root (1848–present) we have learned ecumenism, organization, efficiency, and the importance of academic education.

Having looked at liturgy, and at culture (especially certain values of the Hispanic cultures), we are ready to consider inculturation. This term was used by John Paul II in *Catechesi Tradendae* to mean: "the incarnation of the Gospel in autonomous cultures and at the same time the introduction of these cultures into the life of the Church." Inculturation signifies "an intimate transformation of the authentic cultural values by their integration into Christianity and the implantation of Christianity into different human cultures." (The *Roman Liturgy and Inculturation*, 4). Therefore, inculturation goes beyond liturgy: it is an essential element for evangelization. The inculturation of the Christian life and of liturgical celebrations must be the fruit of a progressive maturity in the faith of the people (5). Inculturation is a two-way movement: 1) it brings to the culture the riches of Christ; 2) and it enriches the celebration with the particular cultural rites and symbols which are in harmony with the gospel and are compatible with the true and authentic spirit of the liturgy ("Discourse to the Plenary Assembly of the Pontifical Council for Culture," January 17, 1987, n.5; AAS 79, 1204).

The goal of inculturation is "to express more clearly the holy things they signify ...so that the Christian people... may be able to understand them with ease and to take part in the rites fully, actively, and as befits a community" (*Sacrosanctum Concilium*).

Where can we bring to liturgy our culture, our life, our very beings? How can a full entry into this communal prayer of adoration sanctify our lives? Fr. Benjamin Bravo, S.J. gives an example from his experience.

During Lent parishioners attached small pieces of paper to a wooden cross. On these papers they wrote the crosses they were bearing in their own life, and in their community. These notes were then burned in the sacred fire at the Easter Vigil. Another year they used the statue of Mary the Sorrowful Mother and pinned to her mantle pieces of paper in the shape of tears expressing the people's sorrows; on Easter Sunday her mantle was transformed by shining stars. Faith and life expressed through simple symbols like these are concrete, cultural ways of manifesting a living, personal, and communal faith.

How can we express more clearly the mystery we celebrate through means of cultural symbols? Liturgy is a symbolic expression of our union with Christ in His praise of the Father by the power of the Spirit. *The Roman Liturgy and Inculturation* (39–43) lists some of these symbols:

- Language (the deepest expression of a culture, of the way we think, of what we value): Translations must respect different literary genres, be understandable and suitable for proclamation; prefer a dignified, clear, current vocabulary.
- Music and singing (congruent with biblical and liturgical texts): Use or adapt a "Mariachi Mass" or other popular songs.
- Gesture and posture (some of which are required for the validity of the sacraments) justify the use of drama, especially in the enactment of Scriptural passages.
- Hand-clapping, rhythmic swaying and dance movements (as prayer, not performance) are wonderful ways of inculturation.
- Art, (colors, vessels, vestments, images), as well as rites (sign of the cross, blessings) and other sensory symbols (incense, holy water, etc.) are of particular importance in making a liturgy welcome a culture. Other Hispanic values that can easily express and enrich our Eucharistic and sacramental liturgies are:
- Hospitality: through the ushers' role, greeting persons around us, welcoming newcomers, the occasional sharing of refreshments (particularly during sessions of RCIA or other catechetical gatherings), and acknowledging birthdays, anniversaries, or achievements.
- Family/Community: it is the nature of liturgy to gather. Include the extended family in gatherings before or after liturgy, encourage unity in responses, singing, listening, silence, posture, and gesture. This can include special

recognition of *abuelitos, padrinos, compadres*. Bless children or other persons or objects during visits or upon request.

- Love for nature: Enrich the liturgical environment with flowers, plants, occasionally birds.
- Religion incarnated in life: mention today's needs and situations in homily/reflection and in the prayer of the faithful. Bring daily life into prayer and prayer to daily living.
- Love for symbols: at the entrance procession (not the offertory) carry decorations (handmade by parishioners); encourage the greeting of peace, and popular symbols such as the baptismal dress, *arras* and *lazo*.
- Celebration of life: sing with a spirit of joy, and active participation; never neglect music at occasions such as the *quinceañera*.
- Respect for the dead: celebrate memorial Masses, visits to a cemetery, the *pésame*. Include people in planning for the *Día de los Muertos* and Good Friday.
- Preservation of Family language: use Spanish in homily/reflection; relate readings to daily life and actual events.
- Punctuality: can be encouraged out of respect for those who arrive on time and, perhaps, have other duties.
- Deep faith: Invite and educate about moments of silence, liturgical spirituality, seeing liturgy as opportunity to pray and to gather as an assembly called by God. We need to see our liturgical prayer as expressing our relationship with God and the sacred.
- Deep rooted sense of history and a treasuring of memories: Celebrate liturgy's biblical roots and Catholic tradition. The idea of celebrating the memory of Jesus should be appealing to Hispanics although many of them may not realize that this is an essential part of liturgy.
- Love for Mary: Celebrate the Marian Feasts with appropriate music, flowers, and/or a special place for the image of Mary. An image of Our Lady of Guadalupe as Empress of the Americas is essential in every Mexican-American parish. Learn and celebrate the Marian feasts of some other groups in the parish.

- Special love for the Bible: Scripture readings are an integral part of liturgical celebrations; encourage people to read the lectionary beforehand, to discuss it in groups, to pay special attention to its proclamation at the liturgical celebration and in the homily/reflection.

Other sacraments also have symbols that are meaningful for Hispanics and are likewise very liturgical. These include the baptismal candle, white baptismal robes, holy water, prayer books, rosaries, a white dress or arm-band for First Communion, bridal veils, the arras and lazo, an extra bouquet of flowers for Our Lady at weddings, vigils, home altars, *novenarios*, somber colors at funerals.

Not many Hispanics are acquainted with the Liturgy of the Hours, but once they get to know it, they love it and use it as at least part of their daily prayer. The Liturgy of the Hours normally includes praying the psalms, reading Scripture, and the prayers of the faithful or intercessions. The psalms speak of nature, use symbolic/poetic language, and express many human feelings of sorrow, anger, doubt, fear, trust, joy, etc. Many of us can appropriate those feelings, and we rejoice when we see them so beautifully expressed in the psalms; it has been said that we Hispanics are a "feeling" people, and personal relationships, even with God, are of great value to us. The reading of Scripture is very important for us, and the selections from the Hours is a rich source of meditation and encouragement during the day. Then we are free in the intercessions to express a litany of petitions for all the needs of our relatives, friends, and neighbors. The Liturgy of the Hours could be a very personal expression in prayer. It could also be used as family prayer at home, perhaps alternating with the rosary. A way to familiarize people with this form of liturgy is to use it during daily Mass or/and at beginning and closing of parish meetings.

Every culture needs to be evangelized in light of the Gospel. Some of the antivalues that may hinder certain Latinos/as from participating fully in the liturgy are:

- Overly privatized popular religiosity which places too much emphasis on devotional prayers. Sometimes people find it easier to express their feelings and needs in this way. Many Hispanics, in particular Mexican-Americans, tend to consider these popular expressions of faith as part of their identity. When they do not see them in liturgical celebrations they may not see themselves as belonging to such celebrations. Hence the need to inculturate our liturgies.

- Humility sometimes is misunderstood as an exaggerated sense of "unworthiness." This deprives many Hispanics from receiving Communion and participating fully in the eucharistic celebration.

- Willingness to respond to needs which sometimes are not that urgent, but people may feel compelled to respond to them rather than to participate in the Sunday eucharistic Liturgy.

- Hispanic liturgical leadership is difficult to experience since the number of ordained Latinos is very small, and other Hispanic liturgical ministers are also few. We need to encourage and instruct more Hispanics to perform these services.

- Freedom for affective expression; for some Hispanics, "liturgy" connotes specific and strict rules or norms. This is true not only among Hispanics but among many Catholics, even clergy! Very few take advantage of the flexibility to use different words and prayers during our liturgical celebrations. It is easier to follow the first option that meets the eye or the shortest formula. We all need to be better educated in a depth of appreciation of what liturgy is.

- Tendency to be traditional can be an obstacle to changes within the liturgical celebrations, especially if the changes have not been explained. In many instances this has been an imposition rather than an opportunity for education. Without continuous and even repeated dialogue and education, the renewed celebrations may seem to be more foreign.

All these ways of inculturating our liturgical celebrations are open to us now. If deeper and more extended changes seem to be necessary, there is a definite procedure to follow in order to "officially" introduce them into our liturgical celebrations. The "Instruction" on *The Roman Liturgy and Inculturation* states: "the diversity of certain elements of liturgical celebrations can be a source of enrichment, while respecting the substantial unity of the Roman rite."

Most of the hindrances mentioned, together with others not expressed here, could be overcome by some clear education and constant explanation. We do not go to liturgical celebrations to feel good or to see something new or different. Definitely we do not go to liturgy to be entertained. We need to learn how a particular assembly (e.g., Hispanics) contributes to the celebration, and what are the attitudes all should have for a full participation in praising and thanking God, in sanctifying and strengthening our lives for the glory of God, and the building of the Kingdom on earth.

Let us not forget that the goal of inculturation is "to express more clearly the holy things they signify...so that the Christian people...may be able to understand them with ease and to take part in the rites fully, actively, and as befits a community" (*Sacrosanctum Concilium*). Inculturation does not mean to make a show of our liturgical celebrations, but to help the members of the Assembly to pray, to be in relationship with God and with one another. Inculturation is not limited to the time of the celebration, but is carried on in daily life. I firmly believe that if we understand better our liturgical celebrations and participate in them with our whole being, our lives will be richer and our celebrations more meaningful. Again, we celebrate what we have lived, and we live what we have celebrated: the Paschal Mystery in the total Christ, Head and members, for the glory and praise of the Father in the power of the Spirit.

Jaime Lara

The
Liturgical
Roots of
Hispanic
Popular Religiosity

In 1950 the Mexican historian Luis Weckmann, gave a presentation at the Medieval Academy of America entitled, "The Middle Ages in the Conquest of America," and developed a theory demonstrating that: "the Middle Ages found their last expression on this side of the Atlantic." Any attempt to understand Latin America must recognize that the spirit as well as the details of medieval society still live in Hispanic cultures. Other investigators have followed Weckmann's example in their study of the medieval quality of Latin American politics, art, architecture, music, missiology and Church organization.

Scholars have shown little interest in the medieval liturgy as it shaped Hispanic consciousness in the formative sixteenth century. This chapter attempts to demonstrate that the medieval liturgy is, in part, what has survived in what we call today "Hispanic popular religiosity." To do this we must ask three questions: 1) What was the late medieval liturgy that passed to the New World? 2) What were the liturgical books brought for the conversion and for the liturgical life of the neophytes? 3) What happened to these liturgical forms after the Council of Trent (1545–63)?

MEDIEVAL LITURGY IN THE NEW WORLD

In Europe of the Middle Ages liturgical uniformity was unknown. Each diocese or region had its own Missal with local variations. This was especially true before the invention of printing because liturgical books were copied by hand. The Eucharistic Prayer, for example, mentioned various local saints or added different intercessions. The section that connects the Our Father to the Communion proper varied quite a bit from place to place, and there was no uniform place or moment when the bread and wine were prepared. The liturgical calendar was heavily laden with commemorations of saints, and it included some personages of quite questionable holiness or historical existence. Thematic masses were common; a Roman Missal of 1474 has a Mass in honor of Images of the Savior, a Mass in honor of the Five Wounds, and a Mass of intercession to St. Michael the Archangel for the demonically possessed.

The effects of the liturgical reforms of Trent were minimal in the New World until the very end of the sixteenth-century. The Council did not begin its liturgical debates until 1562, and copies of the conciliar texts did not reach the Americas until several years later. In addition, diocesan synods had to be convoked to initiate its use. There is evidence that the clergy, especially the mendicants (the first arrivals in the Americas: Franciscans, Dominicans and Augustinians), resisted reform well until the end of the century. Therefore, it is no exaggeration to say that the whole of the first century of the Catholic Americas was a pre-Tridentine liturgical environment.

THE LITURGICAL BOOKS OF THE NEW WORLD

In Spain, from where most of the New World missionaries initially came, a bishop educated at Oxford introduced the English Rite of Sarum to the region around Valencia c. 1470. This rite included a "liturgical dragon," or effigy of a serpent-like creature carried on a pole during the penitential procession of Rogation Days and during Holy Week. The same "draco" appears later in American processions.

Even before the reforms of Trent, European clergy desired liturgical renewal. For example, Archbishop Hernando de Talavera began liturgical reforms in his diocese of Granada as soon as the territory had been won from the Moors (1492). Talavera introduced vernacular hymns for responses in both the Mass and the Liturgy of the Hours. He also fostered what we would consider theatrical pieces during the Mass, as well as "liturgical dancing" during certain processions. It appears that he was moving in the direction of a vernacular liturgy, especially for the sake of the new and plentiful converts from Judaism and Islam. He commissioned catechisms and lectionaries in Arabic for religious education, and required his priests to learn that language. Simultaneously, he encouraged a private spirituality based on the official liturgy. He urged his faithful:

> When you get up after your siesta you should recite Vespers and Compline from the Little Hours of the Virgin, as well as the Office of the Dead, if you have enough devotion. Do this in a place, a quiet retreat within your home, where you have made a clean and well-ordered oratory, so that every time you enter it you may be filled with consolation and devotion.

Here we see the emphasis placed on the "home altar" which has entered Hispanic spirituality. A ritual book used in the New World mandated such an altar, complete with candles and statues, as a requirement for the administration of the sacrament of the sick.

Cardinal Francisco Ximenes de Cisneros, Archbishop of Toledo, also initiated many reforms at the beginning of the sixteenth century. He commissioned new translations of the Bible from the original languages, and made a vernacular homily mandatory on all Sundays. He also had copies of the Psalms and the Scripture readings for Mass published in the vernacular.

There was a revival of the ancient national Spanish liturgy, the Mozarabic Rite. After 1492, its marriage ritual, with the use of the *arras* and the veiling of the couple (what today we call the *"lasso"*), has survived until our own days. The Mozarabic Rite also had a puberty ritual for adolescent boys performed by the bishop. It is possible that such a practice inspired the contemporary Hispanic *Quinceañera* for girls.

Two additional "Mass forms" (I use the term loosely) became popular during the late Middle Ages: what we might call, without any disrespect, Wet and Dry Masses. The first was a form of attending Mass mentally if it were physically impossible to actually do so. It urged one to meditate on the words of the Mass, especially on the sacrificial nature of its re-presentation of Calvary and the crucified Christ present in the host. Several contemporary writers call this a "well-heard, attentively contemplated and well-cried Mass," filled with the tears of compunction, and identification with the sacrificial Victim.

The Dry Mass *(misa sicca)* was an official and liturgically prescribed manner of hearing Mass when either bread or wine was lacking or when, as aboard ship, Mass was forbidden for fear of spilling the elements. The formula is found in a missal composed by the papal master of ceremonies, John Burchardus. The celebrant was to prepare a table with clean cloth and crucifix, and vest in the usual manner. He "read the Mass" up to and including the Eucharistic Prayer, but deleted the words of the institution narrative. He did, however, include an elevation, not of bread and wine (which were not present), but of the crucifix. Thus all could venerate the image of Christ rather than his Eucharistic Presence. We know that both Christopher Columbus and Herman Cortes (the *conquistador*-conqueror of Mexico) had dry Masses celebrated daily on board ship. The surprising thing is that in the New World the friars taught their lay leaders or catechists to celebrate dry Masses when there were no priests available. There are reports of indigenous laymen donning alb and chasuble for the ceremony. Later, Church councils condemned the practice more than once, a fact that indicates that it was very popular, and not so easily suppressed. What it does clearly represent is the late medieval exaggeration of the sacrificial aspect of the Mass. **Looking** at the host (or here the crucifix) was, in the popular mind, considered more important than **receiving** communion. Even in Spain most lay people rarely received communion more than once or twice a year. Unfortunately, this sense of non-participation entered the American experience of Sunday Mass.

But it would be a mistake to think that the medieval altar missals had the greatest impact on the liturgical life of the Amerindian neophytes. It appears that it was not the missal but rather the ritual books for the other sacraments (and sacramentals) that left the deepest and most lasting impression on the converts. Like the missals of Europe, these Rituals show no uniformity. Remarkable differences often show up regarding baptism, marriage, the care of the sick and dying, the blessing of bells, pilgrimages, and the numerous medieval rites for warding off evil.

In the early sixteenth century the Dominican friar, Alberto Castellani, had been commissioned by the Pope to produce a new ritual book for the newly converted Jews and Moslems in southern Italy. Castellani did his research in the best liturgical library of the day, the Vatican archives, and in 1523 he published the *Liber Sacerdotalis*, a practical handbook for priests. It came off the press just as the initial waves of missionaries were leaving for the continental New World; its catechetical thrust toward "Jews and heathen" matched their situation with the Aztecs, Mayas and Incas. A textual analysis of Castellani's *Liber* shows that he copied early medieval monastic practices as well as prayers and hymns of more ancient composition. There are extensive quotes from the thirteenth-century liturgical catechesis of William Durandus, and from the

Order of the Catechumenate (an RCIA) by St. Ambrose (fourth century).

This key liturgical book brought to the New World was better researched, more ancient and more authentic in some ways than what was being used in most of Europe. Castellani's *Liber*, a text still not fully appreciated by most historians and liturgists, was the basis of the *Roman Ritual* issued fifty years after Trent concluded.

The *Liber* was also the basis of two liturgical texts composed entirely in the New World. The *Manual de Adultos* (1540) was the work of Vasco de Quiroga, humanist bishop of Michoacan, at the request of the leaders of the Mexican Church. The *Manual* specified a gentle dismissal of the native catechumens after the Creed while the baptized continued the Mass. On their baptism day the candidates, dressed in feathers, flowers and finery, entered the village in a solemn procession on a flower-strewn path. The parts of the rite directed at natives were spoken in the vernacular (any one of hundreds of Amerindian languages). They were warmly welcomed into the believing community. We know that the *Manual* also contained a Marriage Rite adapted to local customs. Tragically, not one copy of the *Manual* has survived; we know of it only by way of secondary sources.

The second bishop of Mexico City, a canon lawyer, commissioned another ritual book during the conservative 1560s. The Caribbean islands, as well as Peru and the Philippines, also adopted this text. The *Manuale Sacramentorum*, better known as the *Mexicanensis*, was a cut-and-paste job. The editor, a secular priest who had little contact with the vast Indian populations, took sections from the existing rites found in rituals imported from Salamanca, Toledo and Seville. Unfortunately, he all but eliminated the adult catechumenate, and he drastically shortened the beautiful prayer formulas of the *Manual*. Ironically, it is the shortened baptism ritual as it appears in the *Mexicanensis* that became the *Tridentine Roman Ritual of Baptism* issued in 1614. Thus an Hispanic liturgical innovation for the "heathens" in the New World became the liturgical practice of the Universal Church!

We can see the influence of the *Liber Sacerdotalis* on the sacramentals (and thus on popular Hispanic piety) detailed in the text. This is especially evident in the unique but varied forms of

Hispanic processions. Most are circular: in Pied Piper fashion they go out of the Church to round up the faithful, and then bring them back into the building. It is in the *Liber* that we see the origin of the four *posa* chapels still used in Mexican and Andean processions. These are diminutive outdoor stational chapels with altars. There the procession would temporarily halt and rest the statue or the host (in a monstrance). Even today many Latin-Americans construct temporary *posa* altars for Corpus Christi.

The liturgical processions of Holy Week in the *Liber* are based on the nascent liturgical drama of the ninth century. In these ceremonies are found the "Deposito" (burial of the host and/or cross in a tomb structure known as the "monumentum"), the "Elevatio" (removal of the host/cross from the "monumentum"), and the "Visitatio" (ceremony of the empty tomb). We recognize vestiges of this in the Hispanic customs of the construction of the "monumentum" on Holy Thursday, the removal of the corpus from the crucifix on Good Friday, the evening *vigilia* by the casket, and the *Santo Encuentro* or meeting of the Virgin and the risen Christ on Easter morning. It is hard to believe, but true, that Hispanics today have preserved the monastic practices of medieval times! Hispanic "monastic practices" do not stop there. The sixteenth century friars were intent on forming "lay monks" of their Indian converts. Scholars have discovered that the natives learned to asperge themselves and their homes with holy water before retiring for the night; they wore the hairshirt or a version of the monastic *habito* whose ritual blessing and imposition are found in the *Mexicanensis*. It is not uncommon today for Hispanics to don a habit as part of a promise or to use holy water in lavish ablutions.

AFTER TRENT

Hispanic processions on the penitential Rogation Days required the use of the aforementioned "liturgical dragon" who appears to have migrated to the most important liturgical procession of the Hispanic year, Corpus Christi. We know it today in various guises as the slapstick creatures of *mampuchos, tarascas, diablitos*, still seen in the more archaic processions.

Originally performed within the liturgy, the "Dance of Moors and Christians," is today a folkloric tourist attraction: angels and devils do mock battle based on the Book of Revelation.

The *piñata* was, of course, also a biblical-catechetical device. Based on 1 Peter 5:8, it represents the devil who goes roaming about unseen (therefore the blindfold) seeking someone to devour. Early piñatas were monstrous. One strikes this devil with the "rod of virtue" and so conquers and receives the reward of the just (candies).

The "theatrical quality" of Hispanic ritual practice today may indeed go back to sixteenth-century catechetical practices like baptisms that took place during a play about John the Baptist, or to Masses that interspersed liturgical drama throughout the celebration.

Other popular practices are traceable to the *Liber* or similar official texts. The use of blessed palms against the dangers of lightning was a para-liturgical practice found in the Ritual as an exorcism against thunderstorms and hail. There is an exorcism against locusts, a blessing of fire, and of incense and sulfur for use against evil spirits.

The rituals prescribe the wake for the deceased in a *capilla ardiente*, and the decoration of crosses with flowers on May 3, the *Cruz de Mayo*. Likewise, the use of talismans like a cross on the roof top or the Holy Names on a shield is found in these documents. In the liturgical calendar of both the *Liber* and the *Mexicanensis* we find the custom of naming children according to the saint celebrated on the day of their birth.

CONCLUSION

This is not an exhaustive list of the liturgical practices that entered popular piety. Nor does it describe how the missionaries culturally adapted certain aspects of liturgy to the indigenous cultures. Rather, it is an explanation of how earlier liturgical practices lived on after the reforms of Trent.

What today we call "popular" or even attempt to erase in the name of good liturgy was once a part of official Church rituals and missals. They survive for many reasons. One is because they are the ancient practices of the original evangelizers who were often esteemed by the people. Another may be because they were so similar (both consciously and unconsciously) to some pre-conquest rituals of the old religions. Besides, they are colorful and of immediate appeal.

Certainly the post-Tridentine era added additional splendor, pomp, and theological nuance to certain celebrations such as the Immaculate Conception or the Real Presence. Neither Hispanic liturgy nor popular piety has ever been static; the cultural genius of the people and the historical moment enriched each.

This chapter has attempted to show that the medieval culture did not die in the Old World; it took new forms and new life on this side of the Atlantic. Medieval liturgy is the basis of the little-appreciated Hispanic popular religiosity. And that spirituality, the oldest Catholic faith expression in the United States, is worthy of scholarly respect and serious research.

The
Liturgical
Year and
Hispanic Customs

José López

My hometown boasted a social center/dance hall which was simply called *el salón*. It was on the "Mexican" side of town. It was where the social events, celebrations, and religious events were celebrated. What was most interesting was the interior. Along the walls and all around were paintings of Mexican heroes. Our Moms and Dads would explain who they were, beginning with Father Miguel Hidalgo, the first to give *el grito* (the call) for freedom to Emiliano Zapata, the last Mexican revolutionary. In the middle of all this, at center stage, was the painting of Our Lady of Guadalupe. My Dad would point to her and say, "All these heroes...but if it weren't for her..." As children, we knew the meaning of those words. Everything depended on her role in our history.

OUR STORY/NUESTRA HISTORIA

This is my starting point, for history *(historia)* has a double meaning for us: it means both a history and a story. It is essential to take note of this, for we were brought up in a strong oral tradition in story, song, ballads *(corridos)*, and legends *(leyendas)* that told not only our stories of the people, but in essence the history that we hold in our hearts. It was a history not from books but from the people. This history and story not only told of our people, but also of the faith: the stories of the Bible, the stories of the saints, and living stories as they were acted out in the liturgical year: the devotions, the *posadas*, the Holy Week liturgies, etc. All of these need to be taken together, to be lifted up as one history and story of the people. My story, your story, the Church's story continue as *nuestra historia*.

Here I make a practical suggestion. If one is serious about celebrating the liturgical year with any Hispanic group, it is vital to listen to their stories. Whether native-born or immigrant, one has a story. Hispanics from all corners of the world bring to this country wonderful personal stories, faith celebration stories, and the histories of their countries. We have to listen to these stories, these histories, to be able to celebrate with them, especially the liturgical life of the Church. It is one thing to read the history of Our Lady of Guadalupe or Our Lady del Cobre, another to listen to the story as told by those who have lived it. If pastoral ministers do not take the time to know the people they serve intimately

35

through their stories, liturgical life will become sterile, for their will be no context. Every parish, whether twenty-five years old or one hundred years old, has a history, a story.

Another essential aspect of celebrating the liturgical year is that the particular celebrations throughout the country will be different even in the same Hispanic group. The Mexican-Americans, for example, will differ in their approach to the Christmas season. The sense of celebration, the foods prepared, the regional history, all will give different emphasis to the coming of Christ so that if we travel from Texas to New Mexico to California to the Midwest we will find that particularity that gives that people their flavor, *un sabor distincto*.

ADVENT AND CHRISTMAS SEASON

The beginning of the Church year is also the beginning of the most intense time of the year for business and commerce. Thanksgiving, football, and the busiest business weekend of the year are not foreign to the *Hispanos*. The customs that are beginning to take flower can be overwhelmed by the "Christmas season" as business defines it. To the secular society there is no "Advent" season—witness the start of the "Christmas season." The Church attempts to bring some sanity to the world as the hopeful Advent season begins.

OUR LADY OF GUADALUPE

One of the great feasts of the Mexican-Americans is Our Lady of Guadalupe, celebrated on December 12th. It falls right in the middle of the Advent season. With the awareness of the need for a strong liturgical focus on the Advent season and its importance, this feast day can serve well for keeping this focus. In the context of the historical moment of the doomed Indian civilization comes a message from God, in the form of one of their own, *La Morena* (the brown-skinned Virgin), who comes to bring them the Hope of the earth, for she is wearing the *cinta*, a black maternity belt. Is this not what Advent awaits? It is a teaching moment not only for *Mexicanos* but for all Catholics. Is it any wonder that plans begin as early as in the Spring to celebrate this feast? For those first natives of Mexico as well as for us there is so much to learn and teach, to further create an environment that speaks to the Advent season as well as to the Guadalupe celebration. It can go beyond a "Mexican" celebration to a true preparation for Advent.

Following Guadalupe come the many Advent customs. One of the most popular which is gaining more popularity is *las Posadas*, Joseph and Mary seeking shelter. To teach the native people in Mexico, the friars taught them the story of the birth of the Christ Child, reenacting the journey of Joseph and Mary being rejected at several inns before finding room at a stable. So, beginning on December 16, each night the parishioners visit different homes, each home saying no until the chosen home gives *posada*. The chocolate *pan dulce* (sweet bread), and other refreshments are served to everyone. In this way, many of the people are able to participate. The children, of course, love to follow Joseph and Mary, (especially if there is a real, live *burrito*) singing songs, bearing candles, etc. The color, music, and procession again point to the Hope of the people. Even the poorest of the poor see hope.

In the United States Hispanics also share in the celebrations of Christmas, with the presents and meals and visits and homecomings. Some still celebrate the Epiphany or *Los Tres Reyes*, traditionally January 6th, here celebrated on a Sunday. For many Hispanics, *Los Tres Reyes* is the time to exchange gifts, to commemorate the gifts brought by the Magi to the child Jesus. Perhaps this custom may not survive the American customs nor the liturgical change to Sunday.

LENTEN SEASON AND EASTERTIDE

Ash Wednesday (*Miercoles de Ceniza*) ushers in the season of sacrifice and of self-denial. I use these words in the Hispanic context, for there seems to be a grounding in what one "gives up" for the Lord. But it begins with that drawing forth to the ashes on the person. Why is it so popular for the Hispanic community? I suggest a number of reasons. One that seems to make sense is this: It has to do with death. There are two times we usually hear "Remember that you are dust, and to dust you shall return." (*Recuerda que eres polvo y al polvo volverás.*) Ash Wednesday and at Funerals, after the body is lowered and in place, and the people are invited to throw the soil (*la tierra*) on the body while saying the words. For us these naturally go together. There is a sense of our death, not in a fatalistic way, but in the hope of eternal life, as was the death of Jesus Christ necessary for eternal life to be given to us. This bears directly upon the *Día de los Muertos* (All Souls), when we also celebrate Jesus' victory over death. Life and death always go together, one does not have to separate them. To understand this is to understand why a mother or father will insist that the ashes be given to their babies. It is to understand why "Remember that you are dust..." has more meaning in this context than "Repent..." Ash Wednesday, then, not only gathers us in to remember the time of repentance, but also the focus of the death of Christ on the cross and our own death as well.

It is helpful to keep this in mind as the Lenten season takes on its particular devotions. Here too, one can use the stories of the people as to what their traditions have been. One can continue with them, perhaps introduce customs that have been brought by recent immigrants, or introduce other Lenten devotions from our times. It is also during this time that a sound catechesis for all parishioners of all ages needs to take place: That the Easter Triduum is ONE event. One does not choose to go to, maybe Holy Thursday or maybe the Easter Vigil. To participate fully is to enter into the whole Paschal Mystery. While some describe Hispanics as "Good Friday" people, (and for good reason) there is the tendency to join some of the Triduum and not the rest.

HOLY WEEK

From Palm Sunday on, the most sacred traditions of the people come to the fore. Much before it happens, we need to know what to expect, what to offer the people. This is where parishes who know the history and the story of the people will be able to offer ministry at its best. This is where we ourselves as pastoral ministers have to give ourselves into the ministry of the people to Jesus in his hour of need, for they know what is about to take place. There is genuine sensing of the people who know what it is to take up the cross.

Therefore, on Palm Sunday people do not want little crosses made from palms. They can buy those from vendors. They want palms, lots of palms. What good is the story without palms? At one of the churches where I assisted, the head usher told me that the palms would be placed on a table in front, that I was to bless them, then they would remove them immediately, and then give them out after Mass (notice: no procession either). The reason? The people mess up the Church if we give out the palms before Mass! Everything was to be nice and neat. The symbol was to be removed. The whole point is that Holy Week and the Triduum are messy. There is going to be political intrigue, violence, scourging, a crown of thorns, blood, the sorrowful Mother and friends, abandonment by those closest to Jesus, rejection by the people, nails tearing through flesh, the lancing of His body, and agony on the Cross. And we don't want to "mess up" the Church with some palms? Those who remember their own agonies will understand. Those traditions will then make sense to us: the *pan bendito* (blessed bread) on Holy Thursday, the visitation of the seven Churches to keep vigil with the Lord in the Garden, *las Siete Palabras* (Seven Last Words) on Good Friday, *el Pésame a la Virgen* (accompanying the Blessed Mother in the death of her son), and other varied customs. This is the time to have the traditions acted out in processions, in dramas, by youth, children and adults. In San Antonio there is the enactment of the trial of Jesus at the *Mercado,* the carrying of the cross through the streets *(Vía Dolorosa)* to the cathedral where the commemoration of the crucifixion takes place. Hundreds accompany Jesus, increasing in number each year. But also at Guadalupe Church there is the Way of the Cross, each station where a contemporary act of violence took place, such as drive-by shootings or a murder. More parishes are beginning to do these, as is appropriate to each place. Each one will tell it own *historia.*

Sabado de Gloria (Holy Saturday) was an apt name for this day. Older generations will remember that Holy Saturday actually ended in the morning or by noon. Then it was time to celebrate. There were the Easter foods to prepare, the *cueles* (firecrackers), and the *fiesta,* including the dance. With the reform of the liturgy, it has taken a new perspective. But I do not think that for many Hispanics this has translated well. That is why there must be an insistence upon sound catechetical teaching, beginning with the little ones. In some Hispanic communities I have assisted, they have to contend with the dance. In one mission church, the pastor had scheduled a wedding during the Easter Vigil! When I asked the bride why this was, she told me that her mother had married on *el Sábado de Gloria*. Of course, that had happened in former times. *La historia!*

Easter Sunday is the time to rejoice. Again there is a focus on the family gatherings. Hispanics love picnics in the parks. There is the sense of life, of seeing nature in its beauty, and the life of the children especially, as they play, gather eggs, and represent the hope of the people for future generations. These are the ones to carry on the traditions and the story.

ORDINARY TIME

During Ordinary Time there also is much to celebrate in the liturgical year. Each Hispanic group has its particular saints and image of Mary to celebrate. For the Puerto Ricans there is the great feast of John the Baptist or for the Cubans, Our Lady of Charity *(Nuestra Señora de la Caridad)*, or Our Lady of Divine Providence *(Nuestra Señora de la Providencia Divina)*. All of these are hope-filled signs, which focus on God's work in the world. All these belong to the Universal Church, and where one group does not celebrate as much, another does.

Ordinary Time comes to fruition on the two first days of November as we celebrate All Saints and All Souls. One is a day of obligation and, though the other is not, it has its own dignity. *El Día de Los Muertos* is one of the most important days for the Hispanic community. For many, All Saints is joined to All Souls, in that the graves of babies and children are visited on that day, since they are *santitos* (little saints) or *angelitos* (little angels). Flowers, their favorite toys, favorite music, etc. are taken to them. The following day, people spend time—some of them all day—at the cemetery with their loved one. From the ancient customs of the Indians, the families pray, talk with them, take them their favorite food, for their belief was that this was one day they could return to the earth. It is a most solemn but joyful day. It is day to celebrate Christ's victory over death: "Death where is thy sting?" There is a mocking of death as people make skeletons, candy which represents death, *Pan de los Muertos* (bread of the dead), poetry, etc.

One of the customs is to build an *altarcito* (a little altar) where one places mementos and pictures of those who have died. There are also favorite foods, candles, statues or pictures of favorite saints, books, Bibles, etc. Some parishes have begun to build an *altarcito* where all parishioners can also join in honoring the deceased. A remembrance book can be placed to write names in. The *altarcito* is traditionally left up for the month of November. It is one of the most beautiful Hispanic traditions.

These days are also ones of hope because the story of Jesus continues to be told. The Paschal Mystery enfolds all of life in death. For the Hispanic community then, to speak of death is to speak of life, to speak of life is to speak of death. That is why the crucifix is always a symbol of life. We understand that Jesus had to bear the cross, that every time we look upon him there is only hope, that resurrection will come.

LA HISTORIA CONTINUES

There are so many stories in the Hispanic community as there are in all communities of faith. They all converge in the one Story of Salvation. If we can understand our story, then we can understand the story of those who are different from us. To accept my story is to accept your story. It makes us rejoice in each other. As Elie Weisel summed it up: "God loves us because God loves stories!"

Saint Barbara and Saint Lazarus

Juan Sosa

The Book of the Martyrs ("Martyrologium") became for the Christians of the first centuries the first compilation of lives whose commitment to the Lord Jesus became evident through their free surrendering to a horrible death in the name of their Lord. Later on this text was transformed into the Roman Calendar which echoed through the liturgy of the Church the hope of all who struggled to proclaim their faith in persecuted lands and who witnessed to the strength of God in the midst of human weakness. This calendar added to its list, since the twelfth century, the memorial of St. Barbara, virgin and martyr, celebrated on December 4.

The Roman Calendar has become subjected to many changes throughout the history of the Church. These changes have grown out of the Church's need to focus more on the mysteries of the Lord and of Our Lady and the natural increase of the veneration of Saints. This called for the attention of both the universal and the local ecclesiastical communities.

The most recent reform of the Roman Calendar, a result of the liturgical reform of Vatican II, mandated by its *Constitution on the Sacred Liturgy* of December 4, 1962, contributed to certain changes based on the following criteria, among others: 1) to recapture Sunday as the Day of the Lord by eliminating from the Sunday liturgy those celebrations which had been added down through the centuries and which did not reflect the original Church practice of providing the faithful with the opportunity to deepen themselves into the mysteries of the Risen Lord; and 2) to celebrate the memorials and feasts of the Saints by using from now on the day of their death as the date assigned for the faithful to remember them in the liturgical calendar, and not their birthday as had been the custom before. During this most recent reform, December 4, the twelfth century memorial of St. Barbara—and those of St. Philomena, St. Christopher, St. Lazarus and others—does not appear in the Roman Calendar. The new revision substituted St. Barbara for St. John Damascene, a priest and doctor of the seventh or eighth centuries.

Nonetheless, if the life of this saint once grew out of the memory of a Church community which transmitted her story first by oral tradition before she became the subject of an official celebration, her memory continues to vibrate in the heart of the faithful who

43

remember her to this day. The life of St. Barbara, captured magnificently by the symbols which decorate her well known image, continue to remind the faithful that anyone's commitment to the faith must be shown by actions which begin almost from the day of baptism. This truth seems to surface consistently in the story of Barbara, the young maiden of Asia Minor.

A STORY OF FAITH

Barbara was born in Nicomedia, the capital of Bythinia, today Ismidt in Turkey. Here she lived, and here she died toward the year 235 A.D. at the age of sixteen. Her family seemed to enjoy the luxuries of the times. Her father, Dioscorus, was a fervent pagan subjected to the Roman Emperor Maximinus. Barbara received the good education appropriate to young ladies in those days. She enjoyed the company and the tutelage of great poets, orators and philosophers. Among these, tradition recounts, was a disciple of Origen who transmitted to the young lady the Christian faith.

Upon encountering the Christian revelation, Barbara immediately abandoned the polytheistic religion of her family. She felt so attached to the mystery of the most Holy Trinity that she ordered her servants to open a third window on the tower of her household to remember this great Christian truth each day: God is Father, Son and Holy Spirit, one God in three Persons, three different ways of speaking to and relating with the One, True God.

Dioscorus soon became aware of his daughter's commitment to a new faith. He began to dissuade her of these new ideas, first gently. Later, upon experiencing frustrations for not succeeding, he turned her over to the torturers hoping to see her changed back to the old ways. Ultimately convinced that no torment would change Barbara's heart, newly converted to Jesus Christ, Dioscorus claimed the hideous privilege of beheading his own daughter on a hill nearby.

Barbara knelt on the ground and gave thanks to the Lord for opening the gates of Paradise at last. It took only one swing for the sword to sever her head from her frail body. According to tradition, not long afterwards a treacherous thunderstorm with lightning broke loose. Dioscorus was struck and killed by a fiery bolt.

A Christian took her body to Heliopolis where the faithful venerated her tomb and spread her devotion because of the many favors granted by God through her intercession. This site became a place of pilgrimage for many Christians well beyond the years of the seventh century.

Specialists in the lives of the Saints recognized the miracles performed by the Lord through her intercession. Many, while dying, converted their hearts to Jesus. St. Pius V recognized and confirmed the devotion to St. Barbara in 1568. She became known for the devotion of artillery men, and the Spaniards carried both her story and her image to the Americas.

A CONFUSED STORY

Centuries later, in the tropical islands of the Caribbean Sea, the devotion to St. Barbara became confused through the influence of certain beliefs which African slaves brought to these shores from the southeastern coast of Nigeria. Here, on the lands colonized by England, Spain, France and Portugal, these men and women worked as slaves but lifted their hearts in prayer each day.

Tragically separated from their native land, their culture and their beliefs, the slaves looked for a means of identification with their divinities, to experience their nearness and not their distance. In the stories and the images of the Catholic saints, already the basis for the evangelization and catechesis, the slaves discovered that they were not orphans; their gods and goddesses appeared, though seemingly under a new form, to rescue them.

It is a basic fact that during the latter part of the eighteenth and the first half of the nineteenth centuries the efforts of evangelization did not reach the hearts of the slaves; they merely touched them superficially. Set against the previous eras, when the slave trade was not as fierce as in this period, priests, religious and catechists shared the revealed Word of God with the slaves and their families so that they could find true freedom in Jesus, the Lord. One of the syncretisms born in the Caribbean among the Yoruba tribe was known in Cuba as *lucumi* ("I am a friend"). Lately, it has reached the ears of many with a more popular name, *la Santeria*, or the confused devotion to the saints.

In the statue or image of Saint Barbara one can read her story. Her symbols speak about her life and death: the sword, a sign of victory; the crown which reminds us of her sanctity; the red tunic which reveals her blood shed for her faith; the tower where she opened her heart to God in silence; and the chalice used by the priest at the Eucharist which points from her right hand to the true reason for her unconditional surrender to the Lord—love.

When the slaves saw these symbols they confused the third century saint with Chango, the king of Oyo, the god of war and thunder of the Yoruba religious worldview. Coincidentally, Chango was perceived as a warrior god who marched to battle with a sword; as king, a crown had been a key element in some of his manifestations; Chango's color is red. Each African divinity, also known as orisha, has a preference for a specific color. This king ruled his people from the tower of his castle. And, finally, he surrendered to drinking with great frequency (thus the cup on the right hand of the image).

We have seen through the story of her life and death that Saint Barbara has no direct relationship to Chango, though at various times, and most recently in the last few decades, she has been seen on a new image in which she mounts a horse, as a warrior on her way to battle. This representation, obviously, is a result of the existing and prevalent syncretism of the saint with Chango.

As Christians committed to Jesus by our baptismal faith, we need to discover the truth that sustains our religious experience. Let us discover in the devotion to our saints their true story and their symbols which can become a source of evangelization for people today. Let us be faithful to their devotion within the Church, so that, inspired by their witness to Christ, we may dare live in full our Christian life today. May this story and its symbols help us discover more the power of Jesus, the Lord, for whom Saint Barbara, the young maiden of Nicomedia, gave up her human life to embrace eternal happiness forever.

LAZARUS THE FRIEND OF JESUS

For years now, many Hispanic Catholics in the United States have witnessed certain beliefs and customs surrounding the figure of Lazarus who is sought for intercession and assistance. In fact, devotees of this saint often wonder about the origins of this strong devotion, particularly among Cuban Catholics who continue to visit the Shrine of Saint Lazarus outside of Havana, and who carry within them the impact of this devotion when they leave their homeland.

DOES ST. LAZARUS EXIST?

The first problem a devotee of St. Lazarus should examine is the one brought about by the very identity of the saint. The answer to the original question becomes simple and direct: Yes, St. Lazarus did exist! He was Jesus' loyal friend, the brother of Martha and Mary, known by all in the small village of Bethany. Lazarus shared an intimate friendship with Jesus; they held a special relationship. We know, for example, that Jesus wept upon hearing of the death of his friend, Lazarus, and that he prayed to His Father to bring Lazarus forth from the tomb into a new life (John 11). How much more would Lazarus weep, then, upon hearing of Jesus' death soon afterwards!

Moreover, Saint Lazarus continues to exist! As a saint, he has been venerated in the Catholic Church through the centuries. From the time Jesus raised him from the dead, young Lazarus dedicated his life to preach the message of his Lord by word and example. Such was his dedication and commitment that, according to tradition, he was forced to leave home with his sisters, under the persecutions of the first century, in order to settle in Marseilles, southern France and an ancient Roman colony, where he became its bishop. The Church guards his tomb there as a dear treasure to all who feel devoted to him. Saint Lazarus, always venerated by the Catholic Church, has enjoyed widespread popularity. He was the friend of Christ, known to some as the Miraculous Lazarus and to the French as the bishop of Marseilles.

IS THERE ANOTHER LAZARUS?

The statue or image of Lazarus that devotees venerate in many urban centers throughout our country does not seem to be the image of the young man from Bethany. On the contrary, the appearance of this Lazarus is totally different; a beggar, covered with sores from head to toe, sustained by crutches, and constantly followed by dogs who lick his sores. This statue, popularly recognized by many Hispanic Catholics, represents rather a character used by Jesus in one of his parables.

This parable, (Luke 16) conveys the story of Dives, the rich man, and poor Lazarus. It is a story of contrasts — the poor and the rich, justice and injustice, punishment and reward. In the story Dives mistreated Lazarus consistently; he would not even feed him from the scraps that fell from the table. While alive, Lazarus suffered greatly because of this injustice, but after his death, he lived happily in the Lord. Dives, in turn, received the punishment he deserved.

By using Lazarus, the beggar, in this story, Jesus attempted to convey a message to His people. He tried to change and soften the hearts of those who had become stiff and selfish and had forgotten God's love for all, but especially for the poor and the meek. Many Hispanic Catholics have confused this fictional character with the real person, known as the one raised by Jesus at Bethany.

People in the Middle Ages attached innumerable legends to the true stories of the Saints. Within a worldview filled with social evils and religious confusions which accredited the devil directly with many of the personal or communal ills of the era, the multiplication of stories and legends about the saints provided a means of protection and intercession for the faithful. Some writers have calculated that more than 60,000 saints were popularly venerated by the people. The Church, in turn, established the processes of beatification and canonization to determine more accurately the intervention of God in human life through the intercession of His saints.

It would not be strange, therefore, to find some of these confused elements surrounding the name and the devotion of St. Lazarus. At that time, the plagues, the overwhelming poverty and the prevailing oppression which the people suffered seemed to have elicited from them a search for effective intercessors before God and humanity. In fact, the Roman Martyrology prior to Vatican II lists four saints with the same name Lazarus: a bishop, whose feast was held on February 11, a monk, whose feast was celebrated on February 23, a martyr, whose feast was dated as March 27 and, finally, the friend and disciple of Christ, the bishop of Marseilles, whose celebration was dated on December 17. In addition to these four names, *Butler's Lives of the Saints* gives us another insight into

48

the power surrounding the name Lazarus. In volume IV, and as a footnote to St. Lazarus, the authors add:

> The military order of hospitaller-knights of St. Lazarus of Jerusalem (still existing in the form of two separate orders, of merit and knighthood, in Italy and France) did not take its name from this Lazarus but from the fictitious Lazarus, 'full of sores,' of our Lord's Parable.

One suspects that this military order supported or was transformed into a community of servants dedicated to the care of the sick, particularly those suffering from the plague or from leprosy, a reality which echoes the physical condition of the Lazarus depicted by Luke's gospel. Interestingly enough, the Shrine of St. Lazarus, near the city of Havana, is located next to a sanatorium for the care of lepers, but managed by the Daughters of Charity since 1854.

IS THERE AN AFRICAN LAZARUS?

In the same way that St. Barbara became syncretized with an African divinity of the Yoruba tribe, St. Lazarus found a counterpart in an African God, known as Babalu-Aye, the owner of epidemics, diseases and the plague as well as their healer.

This African divinity, whose color is purple, must have found an agreeable association with St. Lazarus if the image accepted by (or proposed to) the slaves and their descendants was that of the poor man in Luke's parable and not the brother of Martha and Mary of John's gospel.

Similar to the experience of many in the late Middle Ages, the experience of the slaves in the nineteenth century displayed an enormous amount of injustice and oppression, suffering and death, (although the harshness of the Spaniards toward their slaves could never match the insufferable and overbearing treatment of the British in their colonies). Tolerance, as a word, may describe the Spanish rule over their African slaves; as long as they did their work, they could express themselves in many ways on their own free time .

Under this more tolerant approach, many *cabildo*, or cult gatherings, emerged among the slaves. These may have appeared as secular celebrations to the slave owners, when in reality they became the focus and locus for worship. At these gatherings the slaves surrendered themselves to the power of their divinities (orishas) whom they believed would communicate with them by "mounting" them as they fell into some form of a trance. Babalu-Aye, like other divinities, assumed the personality of someone present in the rite to bring healing and strength in the midst of disease and confusion. As a religious symbol, Babalu-Aye/Lazarus became a gateway toward health and immediate salvation to the devotees of this syncretism, known as *la Santeria*.

LIGHT IN THE MIDST OF DARKNESS

In conclusion, one can respond to the original question of these reflections as follows: Yes, St. Lazarus does exist! However, any devotee of this saint, and of other saints, must approach the Church to look for the origins of the devotion. It is within the Church that the Lord left His power to guide and strengthen all of His followers. The saints, for some, can act both as witness and as intercessors. The Church, in turn, uses Christ Himself, as experienced by the community through the centuries, as the only light that dissipates all darkness and confusion.

If as Christians we move closer to the Church, where Christ meets us through His Word and Sacraments, any confusion about our faith would soon disappear. He wants to be our loyal friend as He was loyal to Lazarus. He wants to carry on a special relationship with us as He did with Lazarus. He also promised to raise us up on the last day as He raised Lazarus from the dead. In Him we find our purpose in such an indifferent and apathetic society. Through Him we come to know the Father and try to live as brothers and sisters in the faith without racial differences or social distinctions. With Him we journey together through life, guided by the Spirit.

The true devotees of St. Lazarus must turn to the Church to find the truth for which they look. St. Lazarus will lead them to Christ and will show them a way of unity in Christ which they will share with other Christians in the community of faith. St. Lazarus will intercede for them so that, in sickness or in health, their lives may be renewed until they meet the Lord face-to-face and share in His Resurrection.

PASTORAL RECOMMENDATIONS

The celebrations of the saints involve a process which includes three stages affecting the collective unconsciousness of their devotees: Anticipation, Celebration and Renewal. The following suggestions are made for priests, deacons, religious and other pastoral agents who have grown conscious of the influence which the popular religiosity of our communities exerts upon the spirituality of the Hispanic family. These recommendations also address the needs of the devotees of the saints.

ANTICIPATION

1. At least two weeks prior to the celebration of the saint's Feast Day, the assembly begins to anticipate the celebration by getting involved in certain preparations. Due to the complexity of the ordinary life of society today, it is convenient to begin such preparations almost two months prior to the date on which the event itself is to be held.

2. During this period the Parish Liturgical Committee, or those coordinating this event, should meet several times to plan it. Part of the planning should include the Committee's reflections and dialogue about the impact of the feast itself in the community:

   a) Why is this feast so important?

   b) What does this feast mean for the members of the community who have resided in this country for a long time as distinct from those who have recently arrived?

   c) How can we better prepare the religious moments which precede the great celebration of this feast?

3. The Committee should dialogue about the liturgical celebration of the feast, its domestic celebrations, the use of texts, music and ministers who can assist during the Feast Day.

4. It is highly recommended that Triduums or Novenas be held as prayerful moments which can prepare the devotees to encounter Jesus at the main celebration of this event which should be the Eucharist. These Triduums or

Novenas may be held in the Church or in the homes of the devotees who, as small communities of believers, assemble with great devotion. In the case of St. Barbara's Feast Day, just as that of St. Lazarus, its preparation must include a catechetical process about the symbols which decorate the image and which communicate the story of the saint.

SAINT BARBARA

a) Why is there a crown on the head of St. Barbara?
• As a sign of her holiness and her closeness to God in eternity.

b) What does the red cape or tunic on her body mean?
• The blood which she shed at her martyrdom.

c) Why is there a tower next to the image of the saint?
• To show the site of her imprisonment and, at the same time, to assist us in remembering the three windows which inspired her to think about the Trinity.

d) What is the meaning of the sword next to the saint?
• The way in which the saint suffered death by the hands of her own father.

e) And the cup which the saint holds in her right hand?
• The most important of all the symbols on her image, Jesus in the Eucharist, for whom St. Barbara surrendered her life.

SAINT LAZARUS

a) Why does the saint appear in this image without a robe?
• Such was the way in which the dead were buried during the first century A.D.; it also shows St. Lazarus' dependency upon Jesus, his constant friend, and not on material things.

b) What scene does this image communicate or describe?
• The return of St. Lazarus from the dead to a new life; it happened in Bethany, near Jerusalem, four days after his burial, when his friend Jesus arrived and, upon the persistent plea of Lazarus' sisters, Martha and Mary, Jesus brought him to life. (Read chapter 11 of the Gospel of St. John). And the hands which appear before the image? These are the hands of Jesus Himself who calls us all, as He called Lazarus, to renew our lives with his help.

CELEBRATION

Despite the Novena or Triduum which may prepare the assembly to celebrate adequately the feast of a specific saint, we recommend that close attention be given to two other special moments: the Vigil which is held the night prior to the Feast Day itself, and the Eucharist, the major celebration of any Feast Day.

1. The Vigil of the Feast Day is a special moment which anticipates the attention which the devotees of the Saints render to the actual date of the Feast Day.

2. At the celebration of the Eucharist, the major celebration of the feast, all must adhere to the norms approved by the Holy See and the Bishops' Conference, for these norms serve to guide the liturgical celebrations of our Catholic communities.

   a) Preferably, the feast of the saint must be celebrated on the actual date designated by the liturgical calendar or by the popular devotion of its devotees; it should not be transferred to the Sunday before or after this date.

   b) Only the diocesan bishop may grant permission for the transfer of a memorial or a feast of the Church from a weekday to a Sunday in Ordinary Time. If this memorial or feast falls on a Sunday, it is important the community keep the prayers of the Sunday Mass and the readings of the day because of the preeminent place which Sunday holds over any other local or popular celebration. Nonetheless, this Sunday celebration may include: a procession with the image of the Saint, a brief introduction with the history of the Saint that may emphasize his/her virtues as a disciple of Jesus, appropriate songs which carry the theme of 'Christian witnessing' and/or being part of the 'communion of saints,' as well as specific gestures which involve the assembly in this celebration, especially at its conclusion.

RENEWAL

In the spirit of evangelization to which the Church currently calls us, the feasts of the saints cannot merely conclude with a liturgical celebration. Liturgy must commit the assembly to social action. For this reason, the coordinators or planners of this religious event need to raise the consciousness of the faithful to the commitment they must make through dialogue and action:

1. What does the celebration of the feast calls us to do?
2. What is the commitment to which we are called through the story and the symbols of these saints?
3. The feast of Saint Barbara can lead us to reflect upon and to work with:
   a) The youth who search for the Lord.
   b) The members of a family who cannot understand one another.
   c) The prevalent domestic violence.
   d) The price we must pay to live as Christian in society today.
   e) Our surrendering to God through chastity and celibacy.
4. The feast of St. Lazarus invites us to reflect upon and to work with:
   a) The sick, the dying, and the most needy in the community, such as the unemployed.
   b) Those afflicted by an incurable disease, such as cancer or AIDS.
   c) The grieving members of a family who have suffered the loss of their beloved relatives.
   d) The formation of ministers for the Eucharist and for the visitation of the sick.
   e) The communal celebration of the Sacrament of Anointing of the Sick.

CONCLUSION

The lives of the saints reflect God's love toward humanity. They, undoubtedly, indicate that God is present in our world. Through the saints we learn about the stories of outstanding men and women who followed Jesus by living faithful lives according to His Gospel and by suffering death because of its message. Besides performing miracles in their lifetime or after their death, our saints convey to us, through these stories, the most important characteristic of a holy life lived in communion with Jesus and His Church: to proclaim and live out the Gospel of the Lord in society yesterday, today and always!

More Puertorriqueña: an Experience of Pastoral Care with and among Hispanics and Latinos

Sally T. Gómez-Kelley

Traditionally, the Church has ministered **to** Hispanics and Latinos in the United States, rather than **with and among** them. "With" and "among" denote collaborative ministry, or the *"pastoral de conjunto"* of the *National Pastoral Plan for Hispanic Ministry*. However, many Church leaders still continue to regard Hispanics and Latinos as recipients of service. This voids the rich possibilities of collaborative ministries within this community.

Ministry **to** people promotes their objectification. If we believe that Hispanics and Latinos are truly a blessing, it is imperative that our role as effective pastoral agents be the enabling and empowering of their gifts, to be put at the service of building the Kingdom of God-a Kingdom which certainly is culturally diverse.

This diversity has existed from the beginning of our nation. Immigrants from Europe established themselves in this land. They brought with them their languages, cultures, and faith expressions which would shape their prayers, rituals, and ways of living.

THE NEED FOR IMMEDIATE RESPONSE

Currently, the largest group of immigrants or migrants are Hispanics and Latinos. This is not going to change soon. Many predict that the agenda for both the government and the Church in the next century will be greatly influenced by the Hispanic and Latino presence. Therefore, we cannot afford to delay our response to this presence any longer.

Hispanics and Latinos are not only here to stay, but are much more resistant to becoming part of the "melting pot" than many non-Hispanics would like. Becoming part of the melting pot is not only a way of assimilation, but by its very nature it destroys cultural diversity.

A more adequate image, popularized by Justo González, which expresses respect for diversity, is that of a stew, a mixture of various ingredients, each of which retains their essence. They end up complementing each other in flavor and richness. Similarly, in our society and Church, we should strive to celebrate the diversity that is already among us and allow each group to contribute its own flavor to complement the others. Granted, we do not know exactly how the stew will end up, but we trust that it will be good.

EMBRACING DIVERSITY

We need to recognize the challenges which the Church faces. It is easier to deal with uniformity rather than diversity because in diversity we face new and unexpected challenges-which produce fear and anxiety. This fear of unexpected or unknown challenges often encourages otherwise well-intentioned people to propose and enact laws as such "English Only" or, even worse, an anti-immigration agenda such as California's proposition 187.

Demanding that immigrants and migrants speak only English and live according to the standards and values of North America is a clear violation of Christian principles. The Gospels themselves are examples of the cultural diversity contained within the Christian message. They demand not merely a tolerance for diversity, but an integration (contextualized in culture) of the Gospel message into our own way of life.

It is desirable that immigrants learn English, but to demand that they disregard their own language and culture violates their communal identity.

Many of those regarded as immigrants did not actually leave their homes or land but were victims of government treaties and changing borders. Others came from countries where extreme economic hardships and adverse situations have been partially or entirely created by the United States. In reality they are victimized not just once, but twice. This is the experience Virgil Elizondo calls *mestizaje*, a mixture of human groups which gives rise to a new people. Sometimes this *mestizaje* results from violence; that is the experience of most Latinos and Hispanics.

THE CHURCH'S RESPONSE TO THE HISPANIC AND LATINO PRESENCE IN THE UNITED STATES

A significant and concrete effort by the National Conference of Bishops was made by the *National Pastoral Plan for Hispanic Ministry*. This commitment was reiterated at the 1995 convocation celebrating fifty years of Hispanic ministry in the United States.

The *Pastoral Plan* focuses on the needs of Hispanics and challenges all Catholics. It refers to "the Hispanic community among us as a blessing from God." Its goal is to "achieve integration and participation in the life of our Church and in the building of the Kingdom of God." This goal is achievable through a *pastoral de conjunto*, collaborative ministry which will require a tremendous amount of commitment from Church leaders and others in pastoral care. It is certainly going to create tensions and conflict precisely because we do not know what may happen in this "stew pot" which integrates such a diverse group into a Church that has often strived for unity through uniformity.

THE RICHNESS OF THE COMMUNITY

Diversity is not one way. The umbrella term "Hispanic and Latino" embraces a very diverse group of people who share some common experiences: *Mestizaje*, colonization, oppression, marginalization, and faith expressions and rituals not recognized by the institutional Church. Their journeys have led to the crossing of oceans and continental borders in search of a better, more prosperous life for self and family. But they have encountered prejudice and rejection. As a *pueblo* (people) they have suffered rejection of their cultural values: family, *fiesta* and community.

While they share some common experiences, there are also very definite differences among Hispanics and Latinos. These differences, derived from unique cultural and ethnic heritages based on diverse geographical locations, and particularly expressed in music, food, and prayer, manifest themselves in distinct attitudes about or responses to life, God, and family. We should, then, expect a variety of different expressions from the Hispanic and Latino communities originating in the Caribbean, Mexico, and South and Central America.

In order to be effective pastoral agents and truly engage in a *pastoral de conjunto*, it is necessary that we know the history of those we are ministering *with and among*. This history, though, must be nuanced by the particular stories of the persons we journey with in ministry, and is much like putting flesh on bones.

PERSONAL EXPERIENCE

In my own journey, I have come to understand the importance of storytelling, an innate, interpersonal dynamic that reveals truth. Jesus did this well.

My journey among these diverse peoples has made me more reflective and critical about my own history, culture, and faith development. I have come to know better who I am in light of their life experiences as told through the stories we have shared. These stories have challenged me to be more and more what I believe God intended me to be: a *Puertorriqueña* in the United States. And the best part is that I am still in the process of becoming, having known the process of assimilation, acculturation and inculturation.

I have been blessed by ministry with and among diverse groups of people. They have helped me celebrate my own uniqueness by sharing in theirs. We are all subjects in the story God is writing with our lives!

Signs
of the
Times:

Towards a
Hispanic
Rite,
Quizas

Arturo J. Pérez-Rodríguez

The spirituality or *mística* of the Hispanic people springs from their faith and relationship with God. Spirituality is understood to be the way of life of a people, a movement by the Spirit of God, and the grounding of one's identity as a Christian in every circumstance of life.

National Pastoral Plan for Hispanic Ministry (No. 16)

A VERY SHORT STORY

I don't know what made me do it. It could have been that I was feeling particularly good that morning and willing to take up a challenge. Maybe it was because saying good-bye to people at the end of Mass had become a little boring. Or maybe it was because I knew that *los viejitos* (the elders) always told the truth. The "new" liturgy was barely ten years old, and I was viciously curious about its impact on the parishioners. We had tried to implement the reform in this community and so, feeling good, or looking for a challenge or just out of an act of trust I asked the old woman, "Cómo le gusta la misa que celebramos cada domingo?" (How do you like our Sunday Masses?)

She responded respectfully, "*O Padrecito*, [translation follows] I like it very much. Now that everyone speaks Spanish I can understand all the words. I like the new songs that we sing. I like to see your young face smiling at us, and the clothes that you wear, they are very beautiful. I like everything." Needless to say I was feeling affirmed, good, content at having done a good job, and yes even smug, when she added after taking a long breath, "But there is one thing *Padrecito*; I cannot pray anymore. " The simplicity and starkness of her answer struck me to the heart. "Something is missing," I thought. She gently and reverently kissed my hand, crossed herself, and left me standing there. *Los viejitos* always tell the truth.

A NEW RITE?

For over twenty-five years we have celebrated the "new" liturgy, the "reformed" liturgy. What have we gained and what have we lost, as a Church, as an Hispanic community? *La viejita* incarnates both questions. We are reminded in the document *Environment and Art in Catholic Worship*, "God does not need liturgy; people do, and people have only their own arts and styles of expression with which to celebrate." Liturgy is for us. It must be our own. The liturgical celebrations are not purely religious or merely rational and intellectual exercises, but also human experiences calling on all human faculties: body, mind, senses, imagination, emotions, memory (ibid., p. 2). *La viejita* recognizes that though we are closer physically to the people, worship has lost a sense of the sacred that puts us into contact with God. This contact with God is also called prayer. The elements of worship, music, language, environment, vesture, etc., cannot bear the full burden of having us "touch" the God of our lives. As an Hispanic community we look to our own sacred prayer traditions, the genius of our *mestizo* culture, and wisdom of the *rezandores* and *viejitos* for what is missing. These are the ways of embracing life, of celebrating our beliefs. These are the "rites" of our Hispanic people. *The New Westminister Dictionary of Liturgy and Worship* defines a rite as: "...a formal act constituting a religious observance... Those whose object is to facilitate humankind's contact with the holy in such a way that it may be preserved and at the same time enter into a relationship with the source of its being..." (p. 468–9).

Father George Stallings raised the question of the appropriateness of having an African-American rite of worship. The question is a challenge to the Church as a whole as well as to the African-American Catholic community. As Bishop Wilton Gregory states, "The issues are larger than the individuals" (*Origins*, September 7, 1989). Gregory goes on to say that the questions raised are "about some of the most profound and complex liturgical issues that Catholics have faced since the Second Vatican Council initiated the renewal of worship over twenty-five years ago."

As an Hispanic people the question is posed to us while we are caught in a cultural dilemma. This dilemma affects the ways, the rites of our celebrations. Allan Figueroa Deck, in his book, *The Second Wave*, delineates one part of the dilemma when he writes, "At the very outset it must be stated that the use of the word Hispanic is problematic. It is an umbrella term that simply does not do justice to the heterogeneity of the people in question."

The diversity exists not only because we were born in different Spanish-speaking countries, but also because there exists a group of United States-born Hispanics who are generally glossed over when Hispanic ministry is mentioned. Gary Riebe-Estrella says that while being the largest portion of the Hispanic community, it is "the least ministered to by the Catholic Church." (Keynote Speech, "The Challenge for Theological Education," CTU Hispanic Consultation, March 2, 1990.) The rites of this "native" non-immigrant group add a special dimension to this that deserves to be more fully treated at another time. This diversity is our strength and challenge. Our universality of origin, language, similarities of customs and traditions, Catholic religious history allow us to share our lives.

Yet as a body our very presence is a challenge of unity to the Church. The bishops of the United States affirm this challenge in the National Pastoral Plan for Hispanic Ministry:

> To live and promote by means of *Pastoral de Conjunto* a Model of Church that is: communitarian, evangelizing, and missionary, incarnate in the reality of the Hispanic people and open to the diversity of cultures, a promoter and example of justice... that develops leadership through integral education... that is leaven for the Kingdom of God in society. (No. 17)

The other part of the dilemma is that the Hispanic community exists within a multi-cultural, multi-ethnic country.

We find ourselves also being challenged by the questions, faith practices and traditions of African-American, Asian, Oriental, European Christians and non-Christians alike. For the first time we experience not only bilingual ceremonies but also multilingual and multicultural rites. From the Hispanic perspective the question should not be raised fearfully. It would seem that there is a Hispanic rite already extant. Again the *National Pastoral Plan* enunciates this when it speaks about its methodology (and underlying theme for the entire plan) as an "expression of the essence and mission of the Church, which is to be and make communion" (p. 28). We could say that this desire, to be and make communion, is our dream. The plan itself is an expression of our spirituality to make that dream happen. Hispanic worship expresses this spiritual orientation in its language, symbol, and gesture. It is within this framework of "communion" that an answer, a way, a rite is found. Our spirituality is the foundation of liturgy. It merits our attention. I would like to posit more specifically the essential elements of Hispanic spirituality that are expressed "ritefully" when we gather in our homes or in our churches to pray. More than anything else I want to remain faithful to the *viejita* whose stark statement lingers always in the back of my mind and in the depths of my heart.

> The spirituality of the Hispanic people, a living reality throughout its journey, finds expression in numerous ways. At times it takes the form of prayer, novenas, songs and sacred gestures. It is found in personal relationships and hospitality.

> *National Pastoral Plan for Hispanic Ministry* (No. 96)

AN EXAMPLE

Jóse was called *abuelo* (grandfather) by everyone, Hispanic, African-American, white ethnic, new arrival, or old neighbor. He was here before there was a neighborhood. He was the welcoming committee as homes were being built and all sorts of people were moving in. The steel mills of Chicago were his livelihood.

He married a neighborhood girl, had children, watched them and himself grow old, and was saddened when the kids left the city for the suburbs. He belonged to the Catholic Church—or rather the Church belonged to him. Even as a young man he was always there, helping, volunteering, praying, living. *El abuelo* Jóse died a few months ago. Silently and spontaneously as people heard the news the procession to his house began. It came from all directions. Babes at the breast, toddlers struggling with shoes, teenagers with baskets of fresh tortillas, women of all ages, and men—all came to the house to embrace in the *pésame*, to offer prayers, to share tears, and to sit and remember the man around the table of his house. His funeral was like his home: a weekday, standing-room-only church full of people. The neighborhood would fit into the building this day. His watch, his cross, his eye glasses were placed on the casket with fresh cut flowers from his yard. That night the *novenario* began. His wife, Lidia, said that she would lead it. And so the same procession that began five days before wouldn't end until the nine days had been completed. This is the way it is done.

When we speak about liturgy, we must speak about spirituality, the life of the Spirit. This is what liturgy expresses, the inner life expressed in an exterior way, the invisible made visible. Liturgy and spirituality are contrasted not contradicted insofar as in spirituality there are "ultimately no rules of the game, only tips of the trade" *(The Study of Spirituality,* p. 6). Whereas liturgy "is a coordinated corporate activity, for which there must be 'rules of the game'" (Ibid., p. 5). Spirituality is born not in a vacuum but into a specific family with its own history, religious history, culture, cultural history, traditions, religious traditions, beliefs, religious beliefs, values, religious values. Unless we respect and touch, with great respect and the fear of God, the spirituality of our people, then liturgy will continue, as it is at times, to be an empty shell that is boring, trite, and unrelated to the lives of the people who gather. The funeral of *el abuelo* Jóse was not that way.

Sister Rosa María Icaza simplifies our task of naming the characteristics of Hispanic spirituality in her article for *Worship,* "Spirituality of the Mexican-American People" (May, 1989). She lists these as gleaned from the *National Pastoral Plan's* section "Spirituality and Mística":

1. A basic and constant aspect is the sense of the presence of God.
2. God is found in the arms of the Virgin Mary. She is at the heart of spirituality.
3. "The seeds of the Word" in pre-Hispanic cultures are still cultivated.
4. Spirituality is expressed in popular devotions and in the use of symbols and gestures.
5. It is also expressed in behavior revealing gospel values, such as prayer and hospitality, endurance and hope, commitment and forgiveness.
6. Faith is kept alive at home through practices in daily life and particularly during the principal seasons of the liturgical year.
7. All celebrations are seen as communal and most of them include prayer, sharing food, and singing/dancing/reciting or composing poetry.
8. Finally, Hispanics seldom pray for themselves but regularly for others. They often request others to remember them in their prayers.

The article develops these characteristics in such a way that makes her work an important reference for anyone treating this theme. (See also Ricardo Ramirez, "Hispanic Spirituality," *Social Thought*, Summer, 1985.) I would respectfully offer the following as nuances on the list just given.

Hispanic spirituality is incarnational, it is body, soul, and Spirit, all united into one. Virgilio Elizondo in *Christianity and Culture* and Ricardo Ramirez in *Fiesta, Worship, and Family* state this in terms of fiesta, where all life is celebrated. *El abuelo* Jóse's funeral was a fiesta/liturgical celebration of his life and death according to the rites of the Hispanic community. One of these simple rites is sitting down to eat together.

Liturgy does not happen without a meal being involved, either before, or more typically immediately afterwards. This meal extends the experience of the Church into the family and completes the act "of communion" that was celebrated. It is a way of owning and embracing the experience. Also, within the concept of fiesta is contained the sense of the physical, the body, and within the concept of body is contained sexuality. Sexuality is what allows us to use our bodies to be intimate with one another.

Sexuality is what gives passion to life and therefore to the liturgy in the way that the gathered people celebrate their life. It would seem that a boring liturgy is an asexual liturgy. True liturgy within the Hispanic community is anything but that. Yet sexuality is also the constant reminder that we are never satisfied, fully or completely.

The hunger for more remains We are fed in the ways that we live and celebrate life. This hunger often finds its expression in the symbols of Popular Catholicism, (see *Popular Catholicism, A Hispanic Perspective*, by Arturo Pérez). These religious traditions, practices, ways and rites are God's way of providing "our daily bread." Yet as the documents of *Medellin* and *Puebla* so clearly remind us, these ways are in need of purification.

There is a need of purification from the practices that have suppressed "the seeds of the Word" but there is also an acknowledgment contained within these practices that God protects us from sin and temptation. "There is no Christian spirituality without a sense of sin," states Segundo Galilea (*The Future of*

Our Past, p. 46). This protection is needed because within Hispanic spirituality evil exits, not in the theological terminology but in the real presence of the "roaring lion" that Scripture speaks about.

Our Christian generation ought to question itself about its sense of sin and about the dehumanization that sin introduces into our lives and into society. A sense of sin is more than a sense of what is good or bad. The latter is ethics; the former is spirituality (Ibid., p. 52).

Sin, culpability, and evil are engaged personally and communally within the Hispanic community. Within the popular practices of *Santeria* and *Curanderismo* are found the ways we seek God's protection. The purification and integration of these rites is needed.

WHAT OF THE SACRAMENTS?

"Soy creyente pero no practicante" (I am a believer but not a practitioner) is a common way that many Hispanics identify themselves with the Church. Official Church ritual, like Sunday Mass, does not necessarily make a person a believer. Faith is characteristically expressed in the Hispanic community when it evokes an activity. To share in a *velorio, funeral, novenario* (wake, funeral, novena) is an activity of faith. It is the way, the rite of acting out our belief in death and resurrection, of celebrating death and holding on to life. It is the same for the other "great sacrament" moments, namely, baptism, first communion, and marriage. These are the activities of faith that draw us together. Reconciliation is seen as a preparation rite for these other moments. The ambiguity of confirmation, in the sense of a rite of passage from childhood to adulthood, seems to be at a critical moment due to the efforts to make it more a sacrament of commitment. What is the activity of commitment? When it is delayed until the later teenage years there are less candidates. The celebration of the *Quinceañera* (fifteenth birthday of a young woman) holds some possibilities, if it could be expanded appropriately and adequately to include young men and the traditional and contemporary roles that they take on as providers and protectors, companions and partners of the family.

The sacrament of the anointing of the sick, in the people's mind, is still connected with the act of extreme unction, or a rite in preparation for death. The mass anointings of the elderly lessen this connection but do not eliminate it. The sacrament of holy orders is remote to the community since there are rare moments that it is celebrated or witnessed. It would seem that the Permanent Diaconate is the extent of this moment for the Hispanic community. Where there is an activity of faith, people naturally gather.

Hispanic spirituality is more ascetical than mystical. This does not eliminate one for the other. We can say that asceticism is the organization of life around the cross whereas mysticism is the experience of the unity of God with Jesus in the Holy Spirit. In its development we find a time when the "Spanish mysticism of the sixteenth century emphasized the humanity of Jesus Christ, especially Christ crucified." ("Hispanic Spirituality," Ricardo Ramirez, *Social Thought*, Summer, 1985.) Could it be for this reason that the cross still dominates over the Resurrection, Good Friday still draws more people than Easter Sunday? (Some would say that the fruits of current pastoral ministry are the rise in the number of persons now coming to Easter Sunday Mass.)

The ascetical practices of the Mendicant Orders (Franciscans, Dominicans, Augustinians) at the time of the conquest, the corresponding sufferings that accompanied it, and the actual and present day poverty of many Hispanic people play an influential role within the spirituality and worship of our community. Ascetical practices such as fasting, pilgrimages, and promises, are simple examples of how asceticism is woven into the fabric of Hispanic life.

The practices of Popular Catholicism become the "language" for celebration insofar as these practices allow us to express in an outward fashion what we experience internally. The practices of Popular Catholicism are both the spirituality of the Hispanic community as well as the way, the rites of celebrating that spirituality every time we gather.

It is my contention that there already exists a Rite of Hispanic worship. It began at the time of the conquest of the Hispanic peoples. It is a living Spirit of worship that changes, evolves, and adapts to the reality in which it is lived. As Virgilio Elizondo so often states, there is a new *mestizaje* being born. It comes from the dilemma of our lives, of being a diverse people living within a multiracial, ethnic community. It is a *mestizaje* spirituality that is being expressed in the rites of Hispanic worship. This is an experience that for the Hispanic person and community is beyond words. It would be like describing adequately everything that "home" meant to a person. Is it not the very nature of our interior spiritual life to be "unaware" of the richness of our surroundings? Our exterior, public expressions of faith are "common," "ordinary," and "simple." It would seem that the *viejita* was answering the questions about Sunday worship more wisely than I ever knew. Whatever shape reform takes, Hispanic people will be the primary agents of what is right, of what is rite, of what leads them to the prayer of praise of God. They will incorporate, embody, enflesh, worship. I regret not doing one thing at the end of the conversation with her.

I should have kissed *her* hand.

Ministries
and the
Servant
Community

Timothy Matovina

There is the story told of the Anglo-American couple who on Memorial Day brought some flowers to the grave of their loved ones. They were surprised to see how some Chicanos laid food on the graves instead. Surprised, if not amused, they approached the Chicanos and asked them, "When do you expect your departed to come and eat your food?"

Without even looking up, one of the Chicanos replied nonchalantly, "O, about the same time your loved ones will come up to smell your flowers."

The account of the woman who washed Jesus' feet in the home of Simon the Pharisee (Luke 7:36–50) has some parallels to this story. Like the Anglo-American couple, Simon was surprised by the ritual act he witnessed, in this case the rite of footwashing. Also like the couple, Simon responded to the expression of faith he saw in a condescending way, asking himself why Jesus did not reject this public sinner and the sensual ritual which she performed. Simon then received an unexpected response which revealed his insensitivity to the religious devotion of others, as the Anglo-American couple did from one of the Chicanos they encountered.

For Simon, the unexpected response was that Jesus critiqued his lack of hospitality and approved the woman's footwashing rite. Jesus went on to claim that the woman's rite showed great love and that, because of her love, her sins were forgiven. In effect, Jesus compared the religious practice of Simon and the woman and found her more authentic as a minister of hospitality, as a believer, and as a leader of ritual. The response of Jesus to Simon and the woman provides a useful paradigm for reflecting on servanthood and ministries in the Church.

THE EXAMPLE OF JESUS

Jesus' interaction with Simon and the woman who washed his feet indicates what is authentic worship and who are authentic prayer leaders. Simon and his companions were gathered to break bread with Jesus. But Simon did not even offer a sign of welcome when Jesus entered the house. The woman, on the other hand, celebrated a rite which expressed a profound act of worship. In Jewish and other cultures of pre-Christian times, footwashing was a sign of hospitality. But the meaning of this footwashing with

72

perfume and the woman's tears, hair, and kisses was deeper than a gesture of hospitality. Jesus approved her rite for the great love and act of repentance that it signified and critiqued the table-sharing of Simon as devoid of hospitality. He teaches us that authentic worship is not limited to that which has official sanction but includes any prayer or ritual which expresses love for God, demonstrates a radical desire to be intimately united with Jesus, and reflects a conversion of heart. And authentic ritual leadership is not exclusively identified with those recognized by official authority but open to all who have a place in their heart to express a people's faith and urgent longing for God.

Simon's judgment of the woman stands in sharp contrast with Jesus' willingness to learn from her ritual leadership. In fact, Jesus was so impressed by her ritual act that he repeated a similar rite at the Last Supper! This willingness to listen and learn from her is an expression of the servanthood which marked Jesus' ministry. The Master was not afraid to use the rite of a woman known as a sinner, nor to learn from one so unnoticed by her contemporaries that even the writers of Scripture did not deem her name worth recording. He did not merely repeat the rite, however, but offered further interpretations of the woman's liturgical action. At the Last Supper, his footwashing was a symbolic prophecy of his imminent salvific death and an invitation that his followers serve one another in imitation of his example. Jesus learned from the woman's rite of footwashing, examined its possibilities and further meanings, and then celebrated it along with the rite of the Jewish Passover. In doing so he enriched the celebration of Passover with his disciples. He also revealed further meanings of the footwashing rite by linking it to the impending paschal event and the call to service in the community of disciples.

When Jesus had preached to Simon and his companions about the experience of the woman's liturgical action, he said to her, "Your faith has been your salvation. Now go in peace" (Luke 7:50). What a sad ending to this encounter! Why didn't the Lord invite the woman to sit at the table with the others? Was Simon in the end not transformed by this encounter, leaving the woman no place at table with him and his companions? Is this why Jesus did not invite her to the table? These questions cannot be answered from

Scriptural evidence, but it remains that the woman recognized by Jesus as an authentic believer did not break bread with him and the others.

MINISTRIES IN THE CHURCH

These reflections on the servanthood and ministry of Jesus and the woman who washed his feet have implications for the shape of ministry. One implication is the need for pastoral agents to recognize the indigenous leaders and existing worship traditions of the communities in which we serve. A good first question for a pastoral minister upon coming to a parish or faith community is, "Who are the leaders of this people's life and worship?" This does not necessarily mean clergy, catechists, liturgical coordinators, or other designated ministers. Frequently those recognized as "pastors" by the local community do not have official titles. Often Hispanic communities will rely on *abuelitas* (grandmothers) or other elders for consolation, counsel, prayer, and community animation. Virgilio Elizondo has stated that, for Hispanics, the *abuelita* has served as "the priestess of the home religion," for "when there were no clergy to minister to us, our grandmothers were around to bless us, to pray for us, and to offer a *velita* (candle) as the sacrifice of the poor." (foreword to Justo Gonzalez's *Mañana*, Abingdon, 1990). In one parish I met a woman named Doña Licha who, though not prominent in parish organizations, led the annual novena celebration of *las posadas* (Advent novena celebrations which reenact the pilgrimage of Mary and Joseph on the way to Bethlehem) among her family and neighbors. These celebrations were the focal point of her neighborhood in the days preceding Christmas. Like Christ who recognized the ritual leadership of the woman who washed his feet, the first step in pastoral ministry is to recognize people like Doña Licha who are the natural leaders of life and worship in a local faith community.

The next step is to dialogue with those natural leaders, seeking a mutual understanding of their religious practice and that of other pastoral agents. As the Latin American bishops said at Puebla:

> We must see to it that the liturgy and the common people's piety cross-fertilize each other…the religion of the people, with its symbolic and expressive richness, can provide the liturgy with

creative dynamism. When examined with proper discernment, this dynamism can help to incarnate the universal prayer of the Church in our culture in a greater and better way (No. 465).

Such dialogue is an essential element of the *pastoral de conjunto* (literally "pastoral of the whole" or "pastoral of the aggregate") called for in the U.S. bishops' 1983 pastoral letter on the Hispanic presence (no. 11), the conclusions of the 1985 III National *Encuentro* of Hispanic Catholics in the United States (no. 4), and the 1987 *National Pastoral Plan for Hispanic Ministry* (nos. 5–6, 17–36).

The best place to initiate this dialogue is in the homes of the people's natural leaders. Bulletin and pulpit announcements are not sufficient. The wisdom and charism of those recognized as leaders by a local community are important enough to be sought by pastoral agents as a primary ministerial concern.

Two extremes are to be avoided in the dialogue with local leaders. One is clericalism or professionalism, that is, using the power of office or professional training to dominate and control. Dialogue with indigenous leadership begins by learning from them and their religious practice, as Jesus did from the woman who washed his feet. Listening to these leaders can enhance Sunday worship in the same way that the footwashing rite enhanced Jesus' celebration of the Passover. For example, in communities where the *posadas* tradition is practiced, the fourth Sunday of Advent provides a good opportunity to incorporate a modified celebration of that tradition into the Eucharist. By including those who lead neighborhood or home *posadas* in the preparation and celebration of that Sunday's Eucharist, the *posadas* and the Eucharist can mutually enrich one another. Practitioners of the *posada* can offer the community the dramatic proclamation of the hospitality offered the pilgrims Mary and Joseph, calling those present to make *posada* in their hearts that Christ might be born there anew. Those charged with ministering at Eucharist can remind the assembly in this Sunday's celebration that, like the holy pilgrims, we are called during Advent (and always) to prepare and wait in hope for the One who comes. The gospel selections for that Sunday are on Mary's role in the incarnation and are conducive to the theme of waiting in hope while making *posadas* for Christ within ourselves. Perhaps it could be stated that the most intimate way we offer *posadas* is in the Eucharist, receiving Christ in the Word, in communion, and in one another. Just as Jesus enriched the Passover and the woman's footwashing rite by celebrating them jointly, so the Eucharist and the *posadas* can mutually enrich one another and the communities of faith which celebrate them.

Any number of elements from the people's religious practices could be incorporated into Sunday Eucharist and other feasts. In Hispanic communities, for example, the practice of children, parents, and grandparents blessing one another could be incorporated into the closing blessing. Particular artistic expressions like the Guatemalan *nacimiento* (manger scene) could be part of art and environment in the appropriate liturgical season. Practitioners of the home altar tradition could be invited to assist in art and environment. Devotion to the saints could be incorporated by encouraging that the people's images be used for art and environment on All Saints Day. The Hispanic penchant for processions could be drawn on for feasts of the liturgical year which call for or are conducive to processions, e.g., Palm Sunday, Holy Thursday, and Corpus Christi. Further examples abound, and are best learned from the traditions of the local community. In all instances, the desire is to enhance appreciation and understanding of the Eucharist and of the community's ritual, above all seeking to unite the community in a sacramental act of faith, worship, and praise.

The other extreme to be avoided in the dialogue with local leaders is the contention that as pastoral agents we have little or nothing to offer those we encounter in ministry. We are of no help if we refuse to learn from the prayer life of the local community, but we are also of no help if we simply affirm all that we encounter in the religious practice of others. A few years ago I was at a wedding in which the groom presented the bride symbolic *arras* (coins). An invocation which frequently accompanies this action states:

> Groom: "Receive these coins; they are a pledge of the care I will take so that we won't lack what is necessary in our home."

> Bride: "I receive them as a sign of the care I will take so that our home will prosper."

This couple wanted to use the traditional *arras* symbol but did not like the implication that the husband was to be the breadwinner while the wife worked at home (especially since both were going to work outside the home, at least for the initial stages of their marriage). After we discussed this concern, they decided to substitute their own invocation for the presentation of the *arras*:

Groom: "Receive these coins as a symbol of the effort the two of us will make to live a simple life in imitation of Christ and the gospel."

Bride: "I receive them as a symbol of the care the two of us will take to share our goods with the poorest ones we encounter on our way."

Their critical use of the *arras* rite recalls the ministry of Jesus, who learned from the woman's footwashing rite but also revealed its further meanings in his own liturgical action. In the same way, pastoral agents are called to offer their reflections on the people's religious practices based on knowledge of Scripture, the liturgical tradition of the Church, and their own life of faith. As Virgilio Elizondo has stated, pastoral agents are called both to "treasure the same culturally conditioned expressions of the faith, and in the light of scripture and tradition purify and ennoble them so that they will more clearly express the glory of God." *(Origins* 10: 206).

Dialogue with local leaders about ritual practices must never lead pastoral agents to forget the centrality of the Eucharist in Christian life. The words, "Your faith has been your salvation; now go in peace" should be an invitation to approach the table of the Lord, not leave that table. How many do we have in our communities who, like the woman of the gospel, have an intimate relationship with Jesus but feel they are not welcome to sit at table with the Lord? How many are there who express a tremendous love for Jesus in their devotional life but do not receive Christ in the Eucharist? Some, of course, are prohibited by Church law, others stay away out of protest, others feel unworthy, or simply do not value the sacrament. Whatever the reason, the result is tragic for us who believe that the bread we break is the bread of life. The woman who washed Jesus' feet left the place where he was about to sit at table; our mission is to struggle so that all God's children will feel at home in the breaking of the bread. Our ministry has as its end opening the doors of the Church and living our communion with all.

The ministries of the Church are in our hands. We are called to be a servant community: A community that recognizes the natural leaders that God has given us, a community that dialogues with those leaders, a community that invites those leaders and all to sit together at the table of the Lord. May our vision be to receive one another as Christ received the holy woman of the gospel. May we work together to realize the dream of being united around one table, receiving together the bread that gives us life. *Nos vemos en la comunión*—Let us see one another in communion.

Presiding in Spanish as a Second Language

Kenneth G. Davis,
OFM, Conv.

All presiding requires a sensitivity to the specifics of a given assembly. During the Gulf war, for example, my parish near Berkeley, CA was composed of both die hard pacifists, and the worried but proud families of soldiers in danger. Respecting the beliefs of both groups, and leading them in a single act of worship, demanded a finesse afforded only after intimate experience with them all.

Presiding, then, not only includes the orchestration of other liturgical ministers, but also the art of leading a particular assembly in prayer. Therefore, the presider must intimately understand the dialectical tensions peculiar to a given place.

Dialect can complicate this dialectic, and cultural clash can compromise this understanding, when an assembly's native language is Spanish, and the presider's is not. This is a common yet unexplored experience in the U.S. Church, and the theme of this essay. Rather than join the necessary but universal debate over who should be allowed to preside, I suggest guidelines for those of us called to do so in a second language (Spanish), but never properly prepared for it.

First, of course, one must learn Spanish well. It is not enough to read the Sacramentary. While this may be an acceptable beginning, after a year or so when a presider reads, "The Lord be with you," people may be tempted to respond, "And with your book." However, I suggest that we do closely follow the text because our assemblies are usually composed of various Latino groups at different stages of acculturation. The ritual is (or will slowly become) familiar to them all. A foray into slang familiar to one group of Hispanics may confuse or even insult a different group.

Respecting the text, however, does not mean being bound to it. Speaking Spanish well enough to be comfortable presiding means that we are free to use eye contact, tone, and gesture to bring the ritual language alive, and invite all to praise and thanksgiving. Second, we must include native speakers in every possible ministry. If they have not been prepared, train them. This is essential in every liturgical ministry, but perhaps most especially with permanent deacons. A native speaker at the side of the presider will serve as an important model for the assembly. A good deacon can not only preach, but can help any collaborative presider pray cross culturally, rather than at cross purposes. I have even videotaped myself presiding and asked Latinos (lay and ordained) to offer a critique. This can be a humbling and therefore difficult exercise, but also extremely helpful.

Third, crosscultural presiders must encourage as much participation by the assembly as possible. I do not mean only the essentials of good singing, common movement, and appropriate prayer responses. Rather I refer to the intentional creation of ways in which the assembly can participate through: 1) remote preparation for the liturgy; 2) celebration of popular rites; and 3) testimony during the Eucharist.

Remote preparation means including people in the planning of the liturgy and also in practice for participation in liturgical ministries. Give special attention to the planning and execution of participative music.

Ideally several small groups should be selected and trained to help plan liturgies. Similarly the other liturgical ministers need to be prepared, coordinated, and included in that planning. Fortunately there is a considerable body of liturgical resources now available in Spanish. These include curricula for training ministers, magazines for planning liturgy, and even the means of supporting people through the dynamics of small Christian communities. Check the bibliography at the end of this book.

Those materials and resource people (e.g., members of the *Instituto de Liturgia Hispana*) can be used to insure a cadre of experienced members of the assembly participates in these essential roles. Money ought not be an issue, especially where quality music is concerned. My experience is that people who feel included and empowered are happy and eager to find ways of paying these expenses. It they themselves cannot they will resort to what I call "fiesta financing." By this I mean the time-honored, community-building techniques of hosting dances, selling food, etc. to raise the funds necessary to maintain a vibrant worshiping community.

One benefit of creating these small groups of ministers is that they can also grow to a level of confidence and sophistication sufficient to evaluate a presider, as explained above. The confidence of the other ministers, and the openness of the presider, are absolutely vital. Only such an atmosphere of mutual respect will provide the opportunity for the presider to learn as well at to teach. Presumably, with a Master of Divinity degree, the presider knows more about liturgical law and custom than the average layperson. Law is an important element, and needs to be taught to others who do not know it. But the people know the customs of their own culture: what ambience is most welcoming, which symbols are most powerful, and when people are most likely to respond to prayer.

Not everyone can articulate these intuitions, certainly not in language common to liturgists. But a good presider knows how attend to the *misa, mesa, y musa* which makes up so much of Latina *mística*. It is vital that non-Hispanics remember that as they have something to teach, they also have much to learn. Not only need they learn, through both experience and study, all that they can about the Hispanic communities they serve. They must give particular attention to expressions of popular religion.

Popular religion, according to Anthony Stevens-Arroyo (*An Enduring Flame: Studies on Latino Popular Religiosity*), is the "underlying beliefs about God expressed in a complex of ... devotions." Hispanic popular religion is the most ancient expression of Christianity in the United States. It is a bulwark of cultural preservation, and a mine of theological richness. For any non-Hispanic who hopes to lead worship in a Latino context, popular religion is the school where he must study, the temple where he must pray, the living library where he must humbly return again and again to steep himself in this cosmic vision of reality and Divinity.

Often liturgical norms appear to clash with these popular expressions. However, there are very few Church laws without exceptions or options. Unfortunately, there are still too many people who think "rubric" means "rigid" or who opine that the people need educating although they refuse to learn anything from people. To them I suggest they remember: "There is a reason the Church has a Feast to the Sacred Heart, and not the Sacred Head."

Monolingual, Spanish-speaking Catholics tend to be immigrants, often with little formal education. Perhaps they should learn English and the documents of Vatican II. But certainly their ministers are at least as able to learn a second language, and to "read" the documents of their culture, i.e., popular religion. If ministers are servants, maybe they have to lead the way in modeling a missionary spirit. If they would truly minister to the people, they must learn to love them as they are. If they do that, then when they lead, people will follow.

Why invite Latinos to offer public testimony? An inherent problem with a non-Latino leading an Hispanic congregation is that the people themselves have no public voice. How can they worship as a corporate body if the person who proclaims that worship does so with an accent or an attitude? No matter how good we are, we are not native speakers nor cultural members of the congregation. Therefore, we must devise creative ways in which the assembly takes on more public, conscious, articulate, inclusive, and personal roles in the celebration.

One of these ways is precisely through the mutual respect and collaborative planning outlined above. When a Latino walks into the Church, he or she should not only be greeted by an (Hispanic) usher, but by sights, sounds, and smells that constitute a Tepeyac experience. At the hill of Tepeyac in Mexico, indigenous Juan Diego encountered the sights, smells, and sounds of his own language and culture in the apparition of Our Lady of Guadalupe. Just as this inculturated evangelization accomplished what over a decade of prior effort had not, so an experience of acceptance as an individual with a particular culture at the door of the Church will open the door of the heart.

Another way is to allow people to witness. This can be done by allowing different people to offer public reflections. It can also be accomplished through drama, dance, and dialog.

I have found young people to be particularly adept to adapting the homily to these kinds of inclusive dynamics. By the way, everything I have said about Latinos in relation to the dominant culture is equally true of Hispanic youth in relation to both cultures. They must be included as agents rather than objects in all ministry, including liturgy.

People can also be called forth after communion, and invited to offer a thanksgiving. The Prayer of the Faithful can be opened to spontaneous petition. Both initiatives work easily in small groups. Large congregations require intentional preparation and good planning to insure flexibility and spontaneity.

Planning seems the antithesis of flexibility and spontaneity, but actually can be the catalyst. First, one can choose and encourage a few people to begin. This avoids embarrassing silences, and stimulates others to follow. And if the first few follow some formulae, this will give others just enough direction to feel sure of themselves, and may inhibit the inevitable person who wants to monopolize. A brief introduction and certainly some later evaluation are needed. But with persistence and planning we can accustom people to more participative and personal worship which will place as much of the liturgy as possible in the hands and mouths of the people themselves.

I believe that Catholic Hispanic popular religion is adapting to postmodernity precisely by becoming more personally reflective, and more exclusively public. The guidelines outlined here are based on that assumption. *Retablos* and *milagros* are still used to give graphic testimony to God's greatness: Personal testimony, however, seems to continue this ancient tradition in contemporary society.

Etymologically, "preside" means to guard. It is the duty of those who preside in a culture not their own to guard against conscious and unconscious liturgical imperialism. Learning the second language, empowering native leadership, and placing the symbols of the faith into the hands of the people are ways of guarding against this mistake, and respecting the various roles which make liturgy truly Catholic.

Crosscultural
Music-Making

Mary Frances Reza

Each summer here in Albuquerque we look forward to Summerfest. It is here that the rhythm, harmony, melody, and movement that formed a people are shared with the whole community. The families of a particular ethnic group come together to experience and share their roots and the traditions of their culture. Different cultures are represented during the festival. There is Native-American night, Greek-Mediterranean night, Hispanic night, Italian night, German-Scandinavian night, Asia-India...and so it goes.

One can enjoy the Bhangara folk dance, Greek dances, or one can spend time feasting on baklava, lamb gyros, bratwurst, or fried plantains. One can move to rhythm and blues, dance a jig or *rancheras*, or enjoy the rhythm of calypso. Even though different languages are spoken, art, food, and music become a universal language. People immerse themselves in the celebrations and begin to recognize cross-cultural patterns, accepting the plurality of cultural expression.

For, the Bishops' Committee on the liturgy said in 1982, "the United States of America is a nation of nations, a country in which people speak many tongues, live their lives in diverse ways, celebrate events in song and music in the folk ways of their cultural, ethnic and racial roots." As we witness the many cultures celebrating their unique events during Summerfest, we notice that music is an important part of the celebration, interpreting the deepest feelings of the human heart. All nationalities and classes who come to these events seem to understand and appreciate the role of music, and through it enter into the spirit of the various celebrations.

CULTURAL MOSAIC

Our cultural mosaic has many implications for the Church. The challenge of how best to respect and serve the diverse cultures that come together to worship at liturgical celebrations has been and will continue to be an ongoing process of learning and growth. Acts 6:1–10 indicates to us that differing cultures have always been part of the church's history, with difficulties arising from it: "Now during those days, when the disciples were increasing in number, the Hellenists complained against the Hebrews because their widows were being neglected in the daily distribution of food" (NRSV). In today's world we take up this ever-present challenge anew, with—it is to be hoped—an attitude that we can learn from and be enriched by various cultural expressions. For us Roman Catholics, liturgical music in a bi- or multicultural assembly can be a wonderful way to grow in sensitivity and appreciation of diverse cultures.

LITURGICAL MUSIC AND CULTURE

The development of liturgical music within cultural boundaries is an important heritage of our Church. Yet, at the beginning there were concerns about the quality or effect that innovations would have upon Church music. In the early Church, there was hesitation about the use of musical instruments because of the prevailing cultural use of music. The early Church wished that there would be no confusion between the pagan use of music for theater, marriage celebrations, and banquets (which included sexual overtones and morally questionable practices) and Christian' religious use of music. Instruments provided a clear dividing line between pagan and Christian music. Additionally, the early Church favored singing *a cappella* (that is, unaccompanied; probably a musical style borrowed from the synagogue tradition), which underscored their desire to keep psalmody—the sung prayer of the early Church—free from instrumental accompaniment. Another context for early use of religious music is mentioned by St. Augustine in "De Doctrine Christiana", a treatise on biblical exegesis. Quoting from James McKinnen's *Music in Early Christian literature*:

> We must not shun music because of the superstition of the heathen, if we are able to snatch from it anything useful for the understanding of Holy Scripture; and we need not be involved with their theatrical frivolities, if we consider some point concerning citharas and other instruments which might be of aid in comprehending spiritual things.

In spite of these cultural sharings, the Roman rite has maintained a tendency to limit the use of instruments and musical style in its tradition.

Certainly, at least since Charlemagne, plainchant was the accepted musical form in the Western Church, with a clear distinction by this time between sung and spoken parts of the liturgy. As Robert F. Hayburn (here and in the following three quotes) states in *Papal Legislation on Sacred Music*:

> Gregorian chant has always been looked upon as the highest model of Church music. It has been the proper chant of the Roman Catholic Church, the only chant inherited from the ancient Father, which she has jealously kept for so many centuries in her liturgical books.

In 1903, Fr. Angelo De Santi, SJ., wrote in a letter to Dolm André Mocquereau that

> In the Gregorian chant the Holy Father Pope Leo XIII has opened a new horizon, has traced a new path, and this is the road that must be maintained. In the chant of the Church we must search out truth and art. These two qualities are only found in the ancient traditional chant, and this change must now be restored.

"Restored" is the operative word here, since—due to new musical arrangements (especially the development of polyphony)—the flowing rhythm of chant has been destroyed:

> In the thirteenth century particularly, secular texts were often inserted into the music of the Church, many times in vernacular, rather than in Latin words. Occasionally the tenor was taken from a secular tune. At times the texts were both secular and French. At other instances, one was religious and in Latin (or Greek), while the other was secular and in French.

Contrapuntal writing, though beautiful and inspiring polyphonic music, had taken chant to a novel level. In a treatise *Scientia artis musicae*, Elias Salamon states

> Let them know this for sure, that they are neither looking for the things which are ours, and which can be seen, nor looking for the things of God, nor for what properly pertains to the art of music, because they do not know anything about it, but rather they introduce novelties.

The Church tolerated the use of polyphony, the new art, but plainchant retained priority.

As Catholic missionaries brought Christianity to all parts of the world, with them they brought Gregorian Chant as the music of the Church. Throughout the history of music in the Latin countries, one reads of the effect of *canto llano* on the development of the musical idiom for worship. Many of the earlier *alabados* retained a chant-like quality.

In the process of evangelization, Church music and instruments for worship have developed gradually within the culture of the people. A good example of this is the "son" in Hispanic music. The "son" is always associated with the guitar. Through a syncretic process this Arabic feature was integrated into the Hispanic culture and, because it was a medium that could be utilized by the *campesinos*, exotic elements were integrated, such as the Aztecan "El Tocotín." In some of the present Hispanic hymnody, one can still find these elements in the rhythms.

In Africa, the Gregorian chants brought by the missionaries from Europe were too foreign for the Africans to sing. Dr. Oketo stated at a Gregorian Chant International Symposia that

> The older generations could not cope with this and were forced to corrupt Church melodies to fit their own African musical rules which they knew so well. Tunes were set to their musical scales and modes. This is how Gregorian Chant melodies and other church hymns came to be changed in Africa.

The African Church did away with Gregorian modes and used the Ancholi pentatonic scales to create an Afro-Gregorian chant. The new compositions contained some elements of African music and some elements of Gregorian chant.

The first missionaries who landed in Vera Cruz in 1523 found the power of music an effective means by which the indigenous people would accept Christianity. Music was important throughout Mexico, Central, and South America, and the southwestern part of the United States in the catechization process of native populations. Though there was an abundance of native music, the Church music of the colonial period did not exhibit native stylistic orientation. European idioms were considered the only models suitable for Christian worship; however, the indigenous languages or local dialects were used. The religious music of these peoples began to exhibit syncretic traits; for example, *alabanzas* and *alabados* were also included with the traditional antiphons, psalms, and hymns of the Church. The Hispanics' *alabados* and *alabanzas* remained popular throughout the continent and were eventually retained as folk songs.

Borrowing from art media to enrich liturgy is nothing new, and it continues in multicultural settings. For example, according to Cynthia Pearl Maul writing in *Christ in the Fine Arts*, the poem "The Inn of Life" has crossed cultures into the Hispanic setting where it has been set to the musical idiom of the community (there are different settings). With the influence of the ritual tradition of the indigenous people, this poem has lived for generations; today it is celebrated every year at Christmas in the *Las Posadas* festival.

Further, the Church has always taken well-known melodies from folk songs or other compositions as settings for religious texts. Many have become part of the church's standard liturgical music repertoire. For example, "All Hail the Power of Jesus' Name," written by Edward Perronet, was sung to the tune CORONATION, composed by Oliver Holden in 1793. "Crown Him with Many Crowns," written by Matthew Bridges, is sung to the old tune DIADEMATA, composed by George Elvy in 1868. The list of these "borrowings" is endless, and it includes some contemporary sacred music.

Gaudium et Spes states that "the Church learned early in its history to express the Christian message in the concepts and languages of different people." Because Spanish is spoken ten times more frequently than any other language and is the prevailing non-English language in thirty-nine states and the District of Columbia ("Census Reports," 1993), our U. S. publishers of liturgical resources have made an all-out effort to provide resources in Spanish, including Hispanic music for worship representing different musical idioms. With bilingual settings, African-American music, Native-American settings, trilingual settings of acclamations (including Spanish, English, and Vietnamese), there is quite a choice available. The challenge is to bring all these idioms and languages together as a life-enriching interpretation of our Christian faith.

EXAMPLE: A WEDDING LITURGY

Recently a young couple asked if I would help coordinate the music for their wedding. They had made all the preparations, all the music had been chosen, and musicians and choirs from their parish had been invited to participate. These included the Spanish choir, the liturgical choir, the African-American choir, and a choir from another parish. From these combined choirs, there were guitarists, violinists, an organist, a trumpeter, and a Djembi drummer.

The music chosen represented quite a cultural mix: Pachelbel's "Canon in D," "Que Bonita," "How Great Thou Art" (which is a Swedish hymn set to a Swedish folk melody, translated to English), the Caribbean "Halle, Halle, Halle," Clarence J. Rivers' "God Is Love," a Spanish "*Gloria*" and "*Cordero de Dios*," "Rain Down" (an African-American swing style hymn, written by Hispanic composer Jaime Cortez), acclamations by Paul Inwood and Marty Haugen, "*Pan de Vida*" by Bob Hurd, Malotte's "Lord's Prayer," Schubert's "Ave Maria," and "As a Deer Panteth for the Water" by Martin Nystrom. (At this point, I'm certain there are mixed reactions on the part of the reader; dost thou panteth or gaspeth?)

The young man (an African-American) and young woman (a Mexican-American) are very active in the church life of their respective parishes. They wanted to be sensitive to the language and the music of the faith community that would be celebrating with them: their families, friends, and members of the parish communities Coordinating at this point really meant making choices work within the framework of the marriage rite in a life-giving way. Coordinating also meant bringing the diverse choirs and musicians together into a cohesive family.

This couple had spent much time and energy in extensive preparation. Their choice of music reflected hymns that were familiar to their communities. The music for the rite was included in a program booklet, inviting all to participate in the singing. Gelineau (*Voices and Instruments in Christian Worship*) states:

> Music is to express the faith and sentiments of the Church by means of signs which the believers can recognize as their own.... Just as each nation speaks a language proper to itself, each culture possesses a certain musical idiom.

By knowing their communities and wanting them to participate, their choices created a cross-cultural experience. By drawing on the diverse cultures, each member of the faith community celebrated in the spirit of his or her own culture as well as that of others.

As the marriage rite developed, their choices worked. While the candles were lit and the parents escorted in, the vocalist sang the "Lord's Prayer." As the wedding ceremony was about to begin, the African-American drummer (wearing a colorful dashiki) entered, carrying the Djembi drum. As he began to play, the groomsmen entered. All present immediately felt the energy with which the Djembi drummer called them to worship. One could sense the sacredness of the drum itself, with all sharing in the dynamism of that African symbol.

A Hispanic classical guitarist and three violinists played Pachelbel's Canon, which was the signal for the bridal party to enter. When they were all seated, the trumpeter, guitarists, organist, and choir began "*Que Bonita*" (How beautiful and pure is the bride, presenting herself unto the Lord). As the bride came down the aisle to meet the groom, the church was filled with the rich and joyful sound of the Hispanic song, drawing the spirits of all gathered to "celebration." When all were in place, the choir and cantor led the assembly in singing "How Great Thou Art." The church was filled with the power of song as they sang with full voice a hymn they all loved. The young couple had certainly made use of the musical idiom that called forth the "active participation of the entire assembly of faithful" (*Sacrosanctum Concilium* (SC) #121). This was true of all the choices made for the sung parts of the Liturgy of the Word and the Liturgy of the Eucharist.

"Respecting and fostering the genius and talents of the various races and peoples" (SC #37) has another dimension: Not only were the musicians and music choices a cultural mix, but they represented different levels of musical capabilities. Thus, it is important not only to consider the various cultures represented, but—if the music is truly to be expressive of everyone present—those who choose music must also take into consideration the skill levels of the community. As we face these many challenges, we learn that our "behavior" in cross-cultural music making can only emerge from sound cultural understanding. In too many instances, cultural differences pervade interpersonal relations, but "the Church has no wish to impose a rigid uniformity in matters that do not affect the faith or the good of the whole community" (SC #37).

In this marriage rite, although there was a mixed choice of music, the integrity of the liturgy was respected, and there was full participation by the assembly. The mutual appreciation and respect among the choirs and musicians, in addition to the willingness of all to sing songs of another culture, helped to integrate well the variety of musical idioms. The cultures that came together did not "fear" to express their emotion and joy through song. As the gospel acclamation, "Halle, Halle, Halle," and, for the presentation of the gifts, "Rain, Rain, Rain," were sung, the entire assembly was swaying and clapping as a moving unity. I recalled a remark made by Thea Bowman, stressing the importance of spontaneity: "It permits us to be in God's presence and in community as we really feel and are." Interpersonal relations comprised an important aspect of this cross-cultural liturgy, making and providing a good guide for the choice of multicultural music.

MAKING RIGHT CHOICES

Because music does play an important role in the process of inculturation and is often used by a culturally diverse body, it is a challenge always to make the right choices. Music is not only closely tied into our culture; it is equally tied into the very expression of our faith. Paragraph 23 of *Music in Catholic Worship* says:

> Music should assist the assembled believers to express and share the gift of faith that is within them and to nourish and strengthen their interior commitment of faith. It should heighten the texts so that they speak more fully and more effectively.

We've come a long way since Canadian Juan Marcos LeClerc first introduced the use of *"la musica de folklore"* in Cuernavaca, Mexico as the musical idiom for the vernacular texts that were being introduced for the first time in Mexico. With numerous arrangements already available, and with so many more being published, the use of these compositions as cross-cultural music varies. Some selections are suitable for worship, others are more properly used for devotional prayer, and others are excellent songs for children. I mention in the following remarks some composers who have a high profile in multicultural liturgies and whose music is frequently used throughout the country. They have published some excellent music; these titles, however, were deliberately selected in order to help illustrate some of the questions that arise regarding some of the bilingual arrangements being published.

"Radiant Light Divine" by Rufino Zaragosa, OFM (published by Oregon Catholic Press) is an excellent example of a cross-cultural hymn. It is very simple and contemplative, an excellent setting for a prayer service. The simple modal melody adds power and focus to the text of the song. Zaragosa utilizes the aeolian mode, and the modal harmonies in this composition vary effectively to reference or capture the style and character of early Church music. The music enhances the message of the English text. The Spanish text can present some problems. The descant presumes that the assembly will understand the meaning of the Spanish in relation to the English text. Making this meaning clear is necessary if the Spanish descant is to have a purpose in the composition. Although most of Rufino's music is in English, he has managed to incorporate chant-like qualities with Latin rhythms, thus creating a "happy marriage" of musical idioms and words.

"*Todo el Día* (All Day Long)" by Donna Peña (published by G.I.A.) is a very singable "call and response" type song. There is a rhythmic and syncopated "calypso" feel to it. It is ideal for children. The harmony is appropriate to the simple structure of the melodic and textual elements. "Todo el Día" is the only text in Spanish, which makes the Spanish text so minimal as to be meaningless; incorporating the Spanish language in complete verses would have made this composition more useful. On the other hand, "*Digo Sí, Señor*" is being used widely. Its complete Spanish refrain or English refrain makes this an excellent choice for bilingual liturgies The music works with the text throughout.

"*Pan de Vida*" by Bob Hurd (published by Oregon Catholic Press) is probably one of the hymns most requested by both the Hispanic and the English-speaking communities, yet it has also sparked some important questions. The issue of language-text switching continually surfaces among Hispanics. Something that is very common among bilingual Hispanics is "code-switching." Social linguists are taking a serious look at the waves of language in society. They claim it is an advantage not to be "stuck" in one language. The human brain automatically knows when to switch to or fish from another language. Some "purists" are giving this phenomenon some serious consideration. However, code-switching is not always understood, and fluent Hispanic speakers sense that the language is being lost or that there is disrespect when one speaks by code-switching. This is often transferred to the musical arrangements. For some this can be confusing if the text doesn't flow from the text that precedes it. From a psychological point of view, the sentence is the optimal working unit of consciousness. If the text is limited, what will be the comprehension? Is the text speaking more fully and effectively? There must be a flow of intended meaning and syntax if the text is to be meaningful to the fluent Spanish-speaker. Those who are bilingual have no problem with language-text switching, and some find this a way of coming to know another language.

"Come by Me" by Al Valverde (published by NALR) is an arrangement in which the text is sound and works well in either Spanish or English with the melody. Adding verses 3 and 6 (whose only text is "la, la, la") is not necessary for the structural integrity of the song, nor do these verses add meaning. Valverde makes a nice transition in style and key; however, the ending of the song is weak. It needs more finality. The English translations of verse 7 (text only; not included with the notation) is awkward and it doesn't fit the melody well. There is nothing to explain how it was intended to be sung. This example is repeated with many English arrangements that force the Spanish translation to fit the melody. In this case it is an English add-on.

Other composers are writing bilingual music that works well in the communities. Peter Rubalcava (published by World Library Publications) and Jaime Cortez (published by Oregon Catholic Press) have some bilingual settings that have become popular. Their music is used widely in the western and southwestern parts of the U. S. For developing cross-cultural music, an excellent resource is the *Flor y Canto* hymnal (published by Oregon Catholic Press). There is a variety of styles with strong texts that express the beliefs of the community. Because hymns are used by diverse constituencies, selections with popular rhythmic interpretation can enrich and help people to enter into a music that has been brought through the ages, some from oral tradition and others from contemporary arrangements. G.I.A., World Library/Paluch, Oregon Catholic

Press, and Liturgy Training Publications—as well as other publishers—have provided an avenue for developing cross-cultural music. As the U. S. bishops have said in *The Church at Prayer*

> We must continue to search for appropriate ways to enrich our liturgies both by retrieving our artistic tradition and using it appropriately, being open to new focus of the artistic imagination, and by utilizing the cultural heritage of the diverse ethnic and racial groups of the Church in America.

Other Christian denominations have been influenced by the Roman liturgical reform. Using the Roman liturgical texts and rites, many are looking for or are commissioning musicians to arrange cross-cultural settings for their services. And excellent example of this is the "White Oak Mass" by Rick Vale, which was commissioned by the Cumberland Presbyterian Church. The entire Mass setting—from the Processional, through the Greeting, Kyrie, Gloria, Opening Prayer, Liturgy of the Word, Credo, Prayers of the Faithful, "Offertory" song to the Sanctus,—is a continuous sung prayer. The Sign of Peace leads into receiving the Bread and Cup. The Agnus Dei, Prayer, and Song of Praise bring the Communion Service to closure The entire musical setting becomes the structure for their Communion Rite, creating a prayerful sense of gathering. Weaving the syncopated Latin rhythm through by using claves, drums, and harp with full orchestral arrangement brings unity to the entire prayer. There is a sense of connectedness throughout.

In the processional, "Sing to the Lord a New Song," The Spanish text "*Canten al Señor un Cantico Nuevo*" was woven into the entire piece, as a complete phrase being sung repeatedly throughout the hymn. It becomes a familiar musical phrase that weaves in and out. The kyrie is arranged with a Latin rhythm and harp accompaniment, using the Greek and English texts, and then moving into a triumphant arrangement of the gloria and then returning to a gentle syncopated Latin rhythm using claves and drums to maintain the rhythm of the Opening Prayer. The musical settings of the Liturgy of the Word are an excellent witness to Vale's understanding of the power of the text, but they are also a witness to the clarity with which the full choir proclaims the story.

Although this is an elaborate musical setting with full choir and orchestra, there is much to be learned from this example. Vale is sensitive to using full phrases of the Spanish text or complete refrains. The Spanish rhythms beautifully accompany some of the English texts. Vale is able to weave Latin, Greek, English, Spanish, and Navajo to create a mosaic of musical unity. The musical setting creates a prayerful sense of gathering for this simple Communion Rite, whose large loaves of Bread and the Cups are the strong symbols. It is also quite a commentary in that, although Hispanic and Native Americans are not members of the Cumberland Presbyterian Church (or if they are—the numbers are low), this faith community works in a place where these two cultures, the Native-American and Hispanic, are the dominant ethnic groups and so are very much a part of the congregation's lives. Singing or listening to these languages and rhythms in prayer is one way of recognizing the presence of these people of other cultures; this is a beginning in the process of establishing communion with these ethnic groups. This piece also shows the important role music ministry has in bringing unity and strength to this Communion Rite. The preparation is a witness to the dignity and sacredness this congregation places on this event.

A RICH HERITAGE

There are many wonderful bilingual settings, and some excellent examples of successful liturgical celebrations. As adequate cross-cultural music is composed, we must also remember that within culture there is a cultural praxis. We are in possession of music that we know has worked through the centuries. Sung prayer must be the voice of the soul, and that soul must understand and be moved by the sounds and rhythms that have formed it.

Multicultural liturgies can only be successful if we have the input and participation of the ethnic groups who have come into our faith communities. Participating in the artistic creativity of another culture often brings an understanding of that culture on its own terms. Cross-cultural music can provide us with both an appreciation for racial and cultural diversity and also a commitment to the commonality that unites all of us in the Roman Catholic Church.

Liturgy IS life and there are two world realities: the need for interdependence and the realization that problems cannot be solved by only one culture in a multicultural nation; we need one another. The Church faces the same realities. We must ask ourselves, "In what way does the Church in its worship give witness to the interdependence of cultures?" Pablo Sosa, at the Hispanic National Pastoral Musicians Association meeting in Albuquerque, stated that "our global perspective depends on where you are from, it depends on what you are doing, what you see, and what you don't see. To move from one point of view to another, our own point of view will be changed and strengthened. We will be able to see new things. These new sights become our own insights, depending on our own experiencing. As we make our own input, these become new images that can serve us better in the liturgy."

If we continue as a monolingual Church in this country, we will be handicapped. The Roman Catholic Church has a treasure house that is waiting to be connected. It is where culture meets culture, language meets language. We, as Church, are rich in language, culture, and tradition. The Church has the gifts to connect the future with the past. As Church, we must be a safe haven or a bridge for all ethnic groups. They must be the contributors, with the Church guiding the process. We must be open to the rich heritage of all the people.

Lorenzo R. Florián

Spanish
Phonetics
for
Church Musicians

As the Hispanic Church in the United States continues to grow at a phenomenal rate, many church musicians are realizing the importance of the Spanish language in liturgy. Not only are there more masses where everything is said or sung in Spanish, but more and more churches are having bilingual services as well. I would, therefore, like to give the non-Spanish-speaking church musicians some phonetic rules to help in the singing of Spanish.

GETTING STARTED

First of all, Spanish does not pronounce the "u" in the word guerra as does Italian. This is also true of the "gui" combination. In the song *"Hoy Me Vuelvo a Ti"* by Lorenzo Florián, we find the phrase: *seguiré*. The word *seguiré* would be pronounced [se-gi-re] not [se-gwi-re]. There is an exception to this rule concerning "gue" and "gui" combinations, but it will always be marked with double dots over the "u." The word *lingüistica*, then, is pronounced: [lin-gwisti-ka]. When you have a "gua" the "u" will be pronounced as a diphthong as in *guardan* from *"Salmo 119"* by Lorenzo Florián: [gwar-dan]. When a "g" is followed immediately by "i" or "e" it is pronounced if it were an "h" in English. In Lorenzo Florián's *"Gloria,"* the word *gente* is pronounced [hen-te]. This "h" sound is also used in the pronunciation of "j." In *"Aclamación del Evangelio"* by James Marchionda, we find the word *Jesús* a number of times. This should be pronounced [hay-sus]. This is true for any "j" no matter which vowel it is combined with. Please note, as in church Latin and Italian, the initial "h" is always silent, as in *habitantes* [a-bi-tan-tes] from Diego Correa and Damaris Thillet's *"Canten a Dios."*

The "s," "z" and "c" before "i" or "e" are pronounced similarly to the "s" of English. In the Spanish of Spain, the "z" and "c" before "i" or "e" are pronounced as the English "th." This is not of concern for the Spanish of the Americas.

The "y" and "ll" in some American Spanish dialects are pronounced like the English "j" as in the word "jam." One example would be the Spanish word for "alleluia": *aleluya*. This would be pronounced [a-le-lu-ja]. This is considered a form of consonant strengthening which is found in the formal speech of most Spanish dialects. The alternative "glide" sound is also acceptable, that is

Florián

the "y" sound in the English word "yes." When the "y" is found at the end of a syllable it is pronounced an "i" diphthong as in the Spanish word for "today": *hoy* [oi]. When "y" is by itself, as in the conjunction "and," it is pronounced as "ee."

THE THREE "R"S

The "r" sound is one that is not to be overlooked. When a word begins with a "r" it is always rolled, as in *risa* [ri-sa] from Lorenzo Florián's "*Salmo 126*." This is also true of any "r" that is the initial sound of any syllable, such as the word *Israel* [is-ra-el] in the song "*Bendito Es el Señor*" by Pedro Rubalcava. When you find a double "rr," this, too, must be rolled, as we see in the word *tierra* [tye-ra] from Diego Correa and Damaris Thillet's "*Canten a Dios*:" Linguistics calls the single "r" that is not the initial consonant of a word or syllable an "alveolar tap." This sound is made by a quick tapping motion of the tip of the tongue to the alveolar ridge behind the upper teeth. This is the same sound that is used in the American English pronunciation of the word "butter." This double "tt" in "butter" is pronounced as if it were almost a "d." An example of this "r" is the word *moradores* [mo-ra-do-res] in the song "*Ciudadanos del Cielo*" by Lucien Deiss. This alveolar tap should also be used when the "r" forms a diphthon with "p," "f," "d," "b," "g," "t," "c," and when it is found at the end of a syllable or word (In formal Spanish, a "r" at the end of a word of syllable can be rolled. But this is not the case with sung Spanish). A few examples:

"pr"– *presentaré* [pre-sen-ta-re] (from the song "*Canten a Dios*" by Diego Correa and Damaris Thillet), "fr"– *frente* [fren-te] (from the song "*Cantemos*" by Pedro Rubalcava), "tr"– *tratar* [tra-tar] (from "*Hoy Me Vuelvo a Ti*" by Lorenzo Florián), "r"– *flor* [flor] (from "*Los Rosales en Flor*" by Lucien Deiss), "br"– *nombre* [nom-bre] (from the song "*Canten a Dios*" by Diego Correa and Damaris Thillet).

PURE AND SOFT CONSONANTS

The "t," "k," and "p" in Spanish, as in French, are considered "pure," so there is no aspiration (extra air) produced after these consonants. Do an experiment. First say the English word "speech." Then say the word "peach." Notice that the "p" from "speech is "soft" (pure) and the "p" from "peach" requires more air in its production. It is the "p" of "speech" that must be used in the pronunciation of every "p" in Spanish. Practice this sound by holding a lit match about three inches from your mouth. Say the Spanish word *paz* meaning "peace." The match should not go out. Now say the translation "peace." The match should go out. It is this "softness" of the "p" in *paz* that is needed in producing the Spanish "t" and the "k." But the "t" has another very important aspect to its production. The tip of the tongue will touch the back of the upper teeth (in English it is further back, the tongue touching the alveolar ridge). Hard (but not difficult).

The "g," "d," and "b" are all occlusives (hard) at the beginning of phrases or following a nasal consonant like "n" or "m." The "d" is also occlusive following "l" as in *el Dios* [el djos] (from *"Esta Noche Es Noche Buena"* by Lorenzo Florián). In other contexts, the "g," "d," and "b" are fricatives (soft). For example, when you find "d" between vowels or at the end of a word it is pronounced similarly to the "th" in the English word "thou." So, as in Diego Correa and Damaris Thillet's *"Cordero de Dios"* we find the word *pecado*: [pe-ka-tho]. But the "d" is occlusive (hard) in *cuando* [kwan-do] (from *"Salmo 126"* by Lorenzo Florián). A "b" between vowels is pronounced by almost touching the two lips together. It is a very soft sound. For example, in James Marchionda's *"Misa de los Niños de Dios,"* the word *alabamos* would be pronounced [a-la-ba-mos].

SUNG VS. SPOKEN SPANISH

In spoken Spanish, the "v" is pronounced like the Spanish "b" and follows the same rules. But in sung Spanish, the "v" is similar to the English "v" as in "victory." For example, in the song *"Canten a Dios"* by Diego Correa and Damaris Thillet, one would say [ben-gan a djos] but should sing [ven-gan a djos].

The "n" in Spanish, as in the word *Señor,* is pronounced like the "n" in the English word "onion." The "ñ" is usually found between two vowels.

The "l" in Spanish is not like the English "l" which linguistics calls a velar or dark "l" (pronounced towards the back of the throat). In Spanish the "l" is pronounced with the tip of the tongue touching the alveolar ridge (the alveolar "l").

Finally, a little bit about vowels. Spanish vowels are pure. A single vowel will never turn into any type of diphthong, as it would in English. We could call all the vowels in Spanish "long." Thus, the "a" is like what we find in the English word "father," the "e" is like the one we find in the English word "they" without the "y." The "i" is like what we find in the English word "machine" but somewhat shorter, and the "o" is like what we find in the English word "November." The "u" is pronounced as "oo" in the English word "food." When "i" or "u," which are considered "weak" vowels in Spanish, are combined with another vowel and do not contain an orthographic or written accent, they will form diphthongs:

"ie"– *cielo* [sje-lo] (from *"La Misa de los Niños de Dios"* by James Marchionda)

"ue"– *muerto* [mwer-to] (from *"Aclamación Memorial"* by Diego Correa and Damaris Thillet)

"ia"– *gloria* [glo-rja] (from *"Aclamación Memorial"* by James Marchionda)

SOME REFERENCES AND RESOURCES

World Library Publications has a good number of quality recordings of liturgical music in Spanish. I recommend that you take the songbooks that go with the recordings and follow along with the cassettes or CDs for accurate pronunciation. We don't just want to sing, we want to sing well, remembering what Saint Augustine said: "QUI BENE CANTAT BIS ORA" (Whosoever sings well prays twice).

Celebrating the Quinceañera as a Symbol of Faith and Culture

Raúl Gómez

The *quince años* ritual, celebrating the fifteenth birthday of an Hispanic, is becoming more popular in the United States. However, many of those celebrating the ritual do not understand its liturgical and theological implications. This chapter focuses on that portion of the ritual taking place in church. First is a description of a *quince años* ritual, then a look at its possible historical roots and cultural significance.

My thesis is that this rite of passage helps the young woman, the *quinceañera*, take on the role of a specifically Hispanic female. It is precisely the role of the *quinceañera* that is essential to the theological significance of this rite. This is because women, as religious leaders in the Hispanic community, are vital in ministering to the religious needs of their people.

A *QUINCE AÑOS* CELEBRATION

The following description gives one example of how to celebrate the *quince años* in a Eucharistic liturgy. It is not a model or norm but represents a typical celebration in the United States. The religious ritual takes place in the parish church at a Mass (often in Spanish) that lasts about 45 minutes, usually on a Saturday afternoon. An entourage of *damas* (ladies) and *chambelanes* (chamberlains) comprising up to fifteen couples process in with the *quinceañera* . Her *padrino* (godfather), *madrina* (godmother), and her parents also participate. She may have an escort. The *quinceañera* dresses in a long, wide-skirted gown, usually white or pink, and the entourage in elegant formal wear specially chosen for the event. During the entrance procession the *damas* and *chambelanes* line up on either side of the main aisle so that the *quinceañera* can pass through them into the sanctuary. In front of the altar are seats and kneelers for her, her parents, and godparents. The rest of the entourage sits in front pews reserved for them.

The Eucharist proceeds as usual until after the homily. At this point the *padrinos* (godparents) may testify to the young woman's Christian virtue, and her parents may witness to their daughter's baptismal commitment. While remaining at her place in front of the altar, the *quinceañera* stands and declares her faith in God. After this, she dedicates herself to God and to the Blessed Mother. Then the assembly stands to join her in renewing their baptismal

105

promises. Signs of faith, such as a medal and a prayer book, may be blessed and given to her. Intercessions follow for the Church, the world, the young woman, and her family and friends.

A special blessing of the *quinceañera* concludes the Eucharist. Afterward, the young woman is presented to the community. The ritual then moves to the next phase, usually a banquet, where she dances the *vals* (waltz) with her entourage and escort.

The origins of the ritual are not clear. There is some confusion as to its meaning and purpose. It is most commonly celebrated in Mexico. Central America, parts of South America, and the Caribbean also observe it. In those countries it is mostly a debut of the young women to high society. In the United States, however, the major group celebrating the *quince años* is middle-class Mexican-Americans. It is not clear why this is so. Consequently, the *quince años* ritual has been a source of much controversy among pastoral agents in the United States. Some complain that the young woman and/or her family do not often participate in church before or after the event. Preparation for the liturgy is time-consuming for the presider, and involves people who seem to have little liturgical experience. Some also criticize its extravagance, especially since it involves the costs of special clothing, hall rental, banquet, and the dance. Lately, extra touches have been introduced, such as renting limousines; this raises the expense tremendously. Examining its historical roots may help place all of this in context.

HISTORICAL ROOTS

Anecdotal evidence suggests that the *quince años* ritual has its roots in the practices of the tribes of Meso-America. The civilizations that flourished there developed elaborate rites of passage for their warriors and maidens. Some claim that the custom probably dates to the Mayas and the Toltecas.

Pre-industrial societies had highly developed rituals. They were the essence of meaningful life itself. A particularly salient example: in times of drought, the Mayas chose a maiden of fifteen years to mediate between the community and the rain god. Having had her first menses, she was fertile. Since the people needed rain to live, they sacrificed the maiden at the onset of her life-giving ability.

After being treated as royalty for a period, they threw her into the *cenote* (sacred well) of the rain god as a propitiation.

The *quince años* may also have roots in the Jewish custom of presenting the young lady in the temple. Tradition has it that the Blessed Mother was presented in the temple at age three. Today Mexicans and some Mexican-Americans, in accord with this tradition, still practice the custom of bringing the three-year-old girl to church.

Perhaps the Spanish *conquistadores* and missionaries brought the *quince años* to Meso-America. These missionaries "baptized" many religious practices of the native tribes, especially those with Christian parallels that they could easily reinterpret. Christian Spaniards had their own rites of passage. For example, the Celtic tribes of the northwest region of the Iberian peninsula developed elaborate fertility rites that connected the virginity of maidens to the control of water, and therefore the welfare of the community: sacrificing the option to procreate was thought to guarantee fertility elsewhere. Generous food and drink as well as dancing and singing marked the ritual meals that were key to the establishment of these communal relationships.

The ancient Spanish liturgy, the so-called Mozarabic rite, had four elaborate rites marking life-passages for baptized male children and adolescents. The first rite took place when parents presented the small boy to have his forelock cut as an act of thanksgiving for his life, and as a sign of hope that he would grow in wisdom. A second took place when the boy went to school for training either as a cleric or for royal service. The third was the tonsure, and took place later if the boy was to become a cleric. The last rite took place when the adolescent had the first hairs of his nascent beard taken off by applying hot wax from the Paschal candle: this celebrated the passage into adulthood. It was also an act of thanksgiving for reaching that stage of life. All these rites refer explicitly to Christian initiation. They all took place after communion and before the dismissal by the deacon. When the Roman Rite suppressed the Mozarabic, many of the latter's rituals seem to have been conserved in popular piety.

In my judgment, the Celtic fertility rites, with their ritual meal and dance, as well as the Mozarabic liturgical rites of passage, suggest that the *quince años* ritual may have a stronger connection to Spain than to Meso-America. Nonetheless, its contemporary expression is like Hispanics: a *mestizaje*, a blend of European, African, and American blood, language, and culture.

CULTURAL SIGNIFICANCE

For the purposes of this chapter, culture refers to the interrelationship of all aspects of a society to a set of ultimate meanings and values. Included in this definition are beliefs, practices, languages, social organization, education, processes of socialization, and ways of living which comprise a worldview that makes life meaningful for the members of a society. Meanings and values constitute culture; rituals embody and form these meanings and values, and therefore, culture.

There is a saying: *"Dime con quien andas y te diré quien eres"* ("tell me whom you walk with and I will tell you who you are"). A similar expression in English is: "Actions speak louder than words." These sayings point to the role actions have in constituting who we are as persons. That is because actions are symbolic: they evoke feelings and reveal values. Actions embody what is meaningful. They are culture. The *quince años* ritual constitutes culture as well. As part of its function in this regard, it seems to express Hispanic cultural values of family and motherhood.

Hispanics get a sense of self, a sense of identity, not because they are self-actualized individuals, but rather from belonging to a family. There is a heightened sense of relationship, and throughout life we teach our children how to get along with their brothers and sisters. They discover very early their relationship to "half the town," not only because Hispanic families are prolific, but because the word *familia* means more than the English word captures. It includes blood and spiritual relatives in the home or in the *barrio*. The closest equivalent in English is "community."

In Euro-American culture, people become members of a family in two ways, through birth and amalgamation (marriage). Hispanics also have *compadrazgo*. It is a form of ritual kinship that makes one an honorary member of the family. Though it has no equivalent in English, it is rendered as "co-parenting" or "godparenting." The *compadre* (co-father) and the *comadre* (co-mother) are the co-parents of the parents, and are also their child's *padrino* and *madrina*. Sacramental events such as baptism formally establish this kinship.

Because they are *god*parents, *padrinos* become an integral part of the family and hold a place of respect. Like any parent, this entails certain obligations toward the *ahijado* or *ahijada*, the godchild. The cultural event of the *quince años* further solidifies this kinship dimension because it is ritualized through the sharing of the expense. In addition, the padrinos' participation symbolically represents the entire church and community.

At the center of the Hispanic family is the mother. As the fount of physical life, she has propagated the family by carrying, nurturing, and protecting the offspring inside herself. She is the symbol par excellence of family. It is the mother who makes one a person: she teaches civility and hands on the faith, values, and attitudes that remain with one throughout all of life. In other words, she is the transmitter of (Hispanic) culture. The worst insult made to Hispanics is an insult or curse of their mother. A sign of her status is that the Hispanic woman never loses her maiden name. She will always retain it, and hand it on to her children, along with that of her husband. Also, when a woman marries, she becomes the owner of the house, and receives the title of *ama de casa* (the "master" of the house). Although she puts her children first, the mother is the center of the family. She has the most influence on a healthy family where power is manifested in loving relationships.

Arnold Van Gennep was the first to identify the sequential order of certain rituals that marked the life-passages of individuals as they assumed new statuses within a given society. He called these rituals "rites of passage" because they were socially acceptable ways to negotiate these stages of life. Often these involve some sort of psychic, spiritual, or physical crisis. Van Gennep also noted that some of the most elaborate rituals dealt with liminal experiences, especially social puberty.

As one of its dimensions, the *quince años* ritual addresses social puberty, that period society provides to its youth for transition from childhood to adulthood. It may be an extended period, marked by many rites, or the amount of time it takes to go through an elaborate ritual. It may actively acknowledge physical puberty or ignore it. Puberty, being the time when a young woman enters the stage of her life when she can bear children, is a wonderful but also dangerous time for her and her family. The physical and psychic changes that are taking place are often poorly understood. Important spiritual changes occur as well. Most importantly, she is to assume the essence of what it means to be a member of a certain culture.

The *quince años* as ritual encodes and articulates these decisive meanings for the young woman and the community that celebrate it. Perhaps this is why the ritual is becoming more popular. Although always evolving, it may be providing a profound way to express and make present Hispanic religious and social values to the greater society. This celebration of social puberty or nascent motherhood gives communal and religious expression to the role of women, especially their value in family and through motherhood.

THEOLOGICAL SIGNIFICANCE OF THE QUINCEAÑERA

Various terms describe the application by ordinary believers of religious concepts to everyday life, e.g., popular religiosity, popular piety, and popular devotions. Sometimes we use them interchangeably. I see them as distinct realities: popular piety refers to a spirituality, expressed through devotional practices and customs, which arises from popular religiosity. Popular religiosity is a way of viewing, interpreting, and applying religious concepts and doctrines that are spiritually and culturally meaningful to ordinary believers. Popular religiosity is an "inculturation of faith," and popular piety a manifestation of this through popular devotions. It is a very diverse and complex reality. Hispanic popular religiosity is affective, resilient, and expresses a keen understanding of God's presence and providence. Women are most often the mediators of Hispanic popular religion.

The *quince años* displays the qualities of popular religiosity: it marshals the sentiments toward the main ritual subject, the *Quinceañera*, who is dressed as a "princess," and who receives an outpouring of love by her parents and guests in the form of gifts and the expense of the celebration. Since there is an effort to get the ritual actions "just right," the *madrinas* teach the entourage how to process and how to perform the ritual *vals* at the banquet; they also offer their expert advice at the church rehearsal of the rite. Going to church is a petition for God's blessing and continued care so that the *Quinceañera* can make her way to the fullness of womanhood that, for Hispanics, includes some relationship with God.

The religious aspect of the ritual can help the *Quinceañera* become aware of her faith and to live out her Christian commitment. In this regard, the young woman is at the center of the event. Participation in the rite reveals that popular piety forms part of her religious sensibility and that her relationship to God is important. The Scriptural readings, the prayers, and the final blessing remind her and those present of God's providential care. The blessing and presenting of gifts serve as signs of this. When women take on major liturgical roles such as reader and Eucharistic minister, this reinforces the emphasis on the feminine. The focus on the Virgin at significant points, in particular at the dedication, contributes to the feminine dimension of the ritual as well.

In the United States though, males have also begun to celebrate the *quince años*. This is contrary to the practice in Mexico and other parts of Latin America. Some advocate this change since it is a "teachable moment" in the faith development of young people. However, in my judgment, the significance of the *quince años* is more than a general opportunity for youth ministry. Perhaps the following analysis will help illumine its significance, especially as a rite peculiar to women.

Traditionally, it has been Hispanic women who have handed on religious customs. They have known the "right ways" to offer prayers, organize feast days, and celebrate rituals. Arturo Pérez, among others, notes that this points to women's central role in Hispanic domestic worship. For instance, the mother sets up an *altarcito* in the home where she prays for her family, living and dead; she leads the household in prayer, and mediates God's presence. In effect, she makes the home a domestic church and she is its pastor.

Hispanic women have had a decisive role in the religious life of their people. That is because they are the actual teachers of values and evangelizers of the people. Nonetheless, they have tended to exercise a leadership that often goes unrecognized. However, it is precisely the *quince años* that publicly acknowledges this historic role.

The *quince años* celebrates the young woman's puberty and thus her potential for motherhood. Its religious aspect reminds her of her call to service (another kind of generativity). The *Pequeño Ritual*, prepared by the Archdiocese of Guadalajara, Mexico, envisions the *Quinceañera* in pastoral or liturgical service. That is because Christian leadership is best expressed through service in imitation of Christ. This Ritual offers an option for the young woman to express the type of service she will perform. The themes of the suggested preparation sessions in this book center on thanksgiving for the life of the *Quinceañera* and her discipleship in the Lord. The recommended scriptures and prayers show that the main reason she has received life is for discipleship.

This all reveals that the young woman is capable of ministerial leadership in the faith community. That is, her gender and age do not prevent her from participating in the church's pastoral ministry. The *Pequeño Ritual* encourages the young woman to be involved in the pastoral work of the Church on both local and diocesan levels.

Taking on pastoral service is a first step toward leadership in the faith community. The *quince años* provides a way to guide the young woman in that direction. It calls her to evangelize by asking her to renew her faith commitment. It asks her to rededicate herself to God and to declare her intention to serve. The woman and her family's desire to celebrate the rite may itself be a sign of her disposition to leadership.

The Virgin Mary serves as the best model of Christian discipleship. She has long held a special place in the hearts of Hispanics. Marian Devotion runs through all sectors of society. Several scholars have noted Mary's role in Hispanic culture and faith. In my judgment, Hispanics link Mary to their own experience of maternal love. This is an influence of the pre-conquest affinity between the feminine aspect of the Divine and the community.

The Virgin Mary has had a powerful impact on the indigenous people of Latin America. Perhaps this is because she represents the maternal face of God. For many Native-American tribes, the supreme deity was both masculine and feminine. The European conquest introduced the concept of a predominantly masculine deity. Mary's femininity appears to have complemented the masculine attributes of God, helping the indigenous people see God's feminine dimension, and contributing to the evangelization of the Americas. Mary's function in this schema is to evoke a motherhood that puts children first, models surrender to God's will, and exemplifies superior moral conduct that reveals Christ's presence.

For members of every class and age-group, Mary has become the model of all women. In particular she embodies motherhood par excellence and reflects all that Hispanics value about mothers. The *quince años* links the *Quinceañera* to God through Christ and to the Virgin by the prayer of dedication. The young woman gives thanks for being the image and likeness of God. She also asks Mary to be her model of what it means to be a Christian woman. The *Pequeño Ritual* indicates this means being a *mujer fuerte*, a powerful woman. Suggested readings from the Annunciation and the Magnificat (Luke 1: 26-55), as well as the various Marian themes, hymns and prayers, all reinforce the idea that Mary presents the maternal face of God. I believe that these elements contribute to the notion of Mary's sacredness as mother. By their association with Mary, Hispanic women evidently share this powerful role.

As a result, the Hispanic mother enjoys high social status. Some see machismo as a reaction to this. Others see the importance of women in the religious realm as a sign of what Ana María Díaz-Stevens calls the "matriarchal core" of Hispanic culture.

The liturgical texts always present Mary only as everyone's spiritual mother. Nonetheless, the ritual combination of the texts, the symbols, the gender of the *Quinceañera* , and the stage of life she is in empower her to take on a special status in the Christian community as a model of what Christian life and womanhood should be. In general, it is to be like the Blessed Mother: committed, nurturing, loving, compassionate, and life-giving. The young woman's participation in the rite also seems to affirm the matriarchal core of Hispanic cultures. For instance, the escort is shunted to the side where he participates only as another worshiper. The *quince años* ritual, consequently, constitutes the young lady as a symbol of woman and mother, the center of the Hispanic world of meaning.

Some observers of the *quince años* rite see the role of the *Quinceañera* differently. They criticize the celebration for placing the young woman on a pedestal, dressing her as a princess, surrounding her with a court of honor, and associating her with the Blessed Mother. This can place expectations on her that may be difficult to fulfill. To some extent this is true. However, this rite, arising from a culture that values life, lifts up the young woman's potential for motherhood to help actualize Hispanic culture. That is to say, motherhood means handing on physical and spiritual life and, therefore, culture. This can be done in many ways whether or not one gives birth to children.

Ada María Isasi-Diáz and Yolanda Tarango, two prominent *mujerista* theologians, help clarify women's role as life-givers to the community. These theologians attribute the fullness of "*imago dei*" to women, though Christian theology sometimes has failed to do so. They reject the idea that women are not made in the image of God: Hispanic women can and do image God as they engage in the lifelong process of becoming fully human. This process includes the struggle for survival, both physical and cultural; it is the main concern of Hispanic women. In effect, Hispanic women image God in their struggle to survive by the sacrifices they make for the welfare of their loved ones, much like Christ: they image God's care and life-giving capacity as Christ who also suffered and sacrificed. Moreover, their personal struggle to survive is a paradigm of the culture's struggle to survive. This experience is expressed in Hispanic religiosity. Because the quince años rite affirms Hispanic culture and identity, the *Quinceañera* symbolizes victory over oppression, success in struggle, and God's continued presence in the community. This is clear in the prayers, the intercessions, the readings and the homily. She and those gathered are offered hope in their own and their culture's fears and struggles.

CONCLUSIONS

Through the *quince años* the *Quinceañera* marks the passage to womanhood, but not just any womanhood: She is becoming an Hispanic Woman. The Hispanic woman plays a very important role in her culture: she generates and nurtures life. It is the mother who hands on values, faith, and identity, and so, helps the culture survive. This is a reason why she is sacred. The *quince años* lifts up a vision of life that reaffirms Hispanic identity and values. The *Quinceañera* becomes a symbol of the God who is accessible and incarnated in human culture. Perhaps this is part of the reason the ritual is becoming more popular. God does and can lift up the lowly, the downtrodden, and the marginalized to be signs of God's presence, action, and blessing. Young women can image God by their potential to hand on life. They are also generative in the leadership of pastoral service they exercise. Because women in Hispanic culture and religion play a decisive role in conveying God's blessing and graciousness, the *Quinceañera* is a symbol of God's action and care.

A reason for this is women's "motherhood potential" and their resultant ability to image to the community God's guidance, care and life-giving capacity. This, in part, comes from their association with Mary, the Blessed Mother, who functions as a sign for the community of the Maternal Face of God. Consequently, the *Quinceañera* becomes a symbol that carries many meanings. Part of what she symbolizes is God's continuing care and blessing of Hispanics who are often a remnant people within the Catholic Church in the United States. The *Quinceañera*, as a symbol of women's struggle for survival, is a paradigm of the culture's struggle to survive. The ritual lifts up core Hispanic values and expresses them. This is an historic and powerful role worthy of this festive, popular celebration.

Bibliography

Doris Turek, SSND
Paulina Hurtado, OP

Bensusan, Guy. "Some Current Directions in Mexican American Religious Music," *Latin American Research Review* 10, (2) 1975.

Davis, Kenneth G. "Misa Juvenil," *Construyendo Nuestra Esperanza* 4 (2) Winter 1991: 3-4.

_____"Out of a Crucible of Culture, Hispanic Liturgy's Coming On," *National Catholic Reporter* 13 December 1991: 10.

_____"Preaching in Spanish as a Second Language," *Homiletic* XVII (1) Summer 1992: 7-10.

_____"A Return to the Roots: Conversion and the Culture of the Mexican-Descent Catholic," *Pastoral Psychology* 40 (3) January 1992: 139-158.

_____"Selected Pastoral Resources." in Allan Deck, S.J., et. al., eds., *Perspectivas.* Kansas City, MO: Sheed and Ward, 1995.

Deck, Allan. "Liturgy and Mexican American Culture," *Modern Liturgy* October, 1976.

Elizondo, Virgilio. "Politics, Catechetics and Liturgy," *Religion Teacher's Journal*, 1976.

Erevia, Angela. "Quince Años Celebration: Celebrating a Tradition," *Catechist*, March 1989.

Escamilla, Roberto. "Worship in the Context of Hispanic Culture," *Worship* 51 (July, 1977).

Flores, Richard. "Mexican: Fiesta People," *Modern Liturgy* 13, 3 April, 1986.

Hanlon, Don. "The Confrontation of Two Dissimilar Cultures: The Adobe Church in New Mexico," *Journal of the Interfaith Forum on Religion, Art, and Architecture.* 91/17 Winter, 1990.

Icaza, Rosa María. "The Cross in Mexican Popular Piety," *Liturgy* 1 (1) (1980).

_____"The Cross in Mexican American Popular Piety." *Liturgy: The Holy Cross.* Washington, DC: The Liturgical Conference, Inc., 1980.

_____"Linguistics: A Bridge to Understanding Bilingual Children." *Bridging Two Cultures*, Austin: National Educational Laboratory Publishers, Inc., 1980.

_____ed. "Oremos." *Los Ministros de la Communion a los Enfermos.* San Antonio: Mexican American Cultural Center, 1985.

 117

_____, ed. *Pastoral Care of the Sick/Cuidado Pastoral de los Enfermos.* Chicago: Liturgical Training Publications, 1986.

_____ "Is There a Place for Hispanic Candidates in U.S. Seminaries?" *Call to Growth/Ministry.* Chicago: National Conference of Religious Vocation Directors, 1987.

_____ "¿Qué expresa el género masculino en español?" *Amen.* San Antonio: Instituto de Liturgia Hispana, 1988.

_____, with Juan Alfaro. *Manual para lectores y proclamadores de la Palabra.* Chicago: Liturgy Training Publications, 1988.

_____ Harvesting the "Seeds of the Word" Among Hispanics in the Rural South. Project with Glenmary Home Missionaries, New Orleans: Loyola University, 1988.

_____ "Spirituality of the Mexican American People," *Worship* (63) 1989.

_____ "The Spirit of Hispanic Worship"/"El Espíritu del Culto Hispano." *Flor y Canto.* Portland: OCP Publications, 1990.

_____ "RICA entre los Hispanos"/"The RCIA Among the Hispanics," *Liturgia y Canción,* Tiempo Ordinario I (10 de junio-8 de septiembre 1990), 5-8.

_____ Contributor and ed. "Hispanic Spirituality." *In God's Vineyard, Lay Formation Program for Hispanic Ministers.* Chicago: Serra International, 1990.

_____ Contributor and ed. *Faith Expressions of the Hispanics in the Southwest,* revised edition. San Antonio: Mexican American Cultural Center, 1990.

_____ Contributor and co-editor *Manual de Facilitadores para Establecer Comunidades Eclesiales de Base.* San Antonio: Mexican American Cultural Center, 1991.

_____ "Prayer, Worship and Liturgy in a U.S. Hispanic Key." *Frontiers of a United States Hispanic Theology,* ed. Allen F. Deck, S.J. Maryknoll: Orbis Press, 1992.

_____ Contributor, ed. and translator, *Prophetic Vision/Visión Profética,* (bilingual publication.) Kansas City: Sheed & Ward, 1992.

_____, ed. *Oraciones de Corazón/Prayers from the Heart.* San Antonio: Mexican American Cultural Center, 1992.

_____"A Program for Formation of Hispanic Leaders," *PACE*, May, (1993): 21-24.

_____"Inculturation of the Liturgy"/"Inculturación de la Liturgia," *C.C.V.I. Communique*, March, (1993).

_____"Catholic = Multicultural," *Today's Catholic Teacher*, 1995.

El Rito de Iniciación Cristiana de Adultos. (the official translation for the United States approved by BCL, NCCB, and Rome), Washington, DC: United States Catholic Conference, 1991.

Sunday Celebrations in the Absence of a Priest/Celebraciones dominicales en la ausencia de un presbítero. Bilingual Edition. Washington, DC: United States Catholic Conference, 1994.

Celebraciones Litúrgicas según el Rito Oriental. Ft. Pierce, FL, 1994.

"Bendiciones compuestas por los Obispos de los Estados Unidos." in the *Bendicional*. Washington, D.C.: United States Catholic Conference, 1995.

Ritual de las Exequias Cristianas. Official translation for the United States, approved by BCL, NCCB, and Rome. Washington, DC: United States Catholic Conference, 1995.

Lara, Jaime, Ph.D. General Ed., *El Leccionario Hispanoamericano para los Estados Unidos.* 3 vols. New York, 1985-1994.

_____, ed. *Environment and Art in Catholic Worship.* Bilingual ed., Chicago, 1986.

_____"Pasión y Poder: Toward Understanding the Hispanic Aesthetic." *Faith and Form.* Washington, DC, 1988.

_____ *La Religiosidad Popular: Imágenes de Jesucristo y la Virgen María en Latinoamérica.* San Antonio, 1990.

_____"Estado Actual del Arte Litúrgico en los Estados Unidos," *Actas del Primer Simposio Internacional de Arte Sacro en México.* Mexico City, 1992.

_____"Versus Populum Revisited," *Worship* 68 (1994).

_____ The Prologue to Santiago Sebastián López's last book. *El Mensaje Simbólico del Templo Cristiano: Arquitectura, iconografía y liturgia.* Madrid, 1994.

_____"The Mirror on the Cross: A Medieval reflection on/in the Mexican atrio crosses," an interactive CD-ROM for Inter-American Institute for Advanced Studies in Cultural History (forthcoming).

_____"El espejo en la cruz," *Anales del Instituto de Investigaciones Estéticas.* Universidad Nacional Autónoma de México (forthcoming).

_____"Introducción para el Lector: Ambiente y Arte en el Culto Católico." *Documentos Litúrgicos,* Chicago (forthcoming).

Matovina, Timothy. *Perspectivas: Hispanic Ministry.* Edited with Yolanda Tarango and Allen Figueroa Deck. Kansas City: Sheed and Ward, 1995.

_____*Tejano Religion and Ethnicity:* San Antonio, 1821-1860. Austin: University of Texas Press, 1995.

_____"Guadalupan Devotion in a Borderlands Community," *Journal of Hispanic/Latino Theology* (August, 1996): 6-26.

_____"Lay Initiatives in Worship on the Texas Frontera, 1830-1860," *U.S. Catholic Historian* 12 Fall (1994): 107-120.

_____"Liturgy and Popular Expressions of Faith: A Look at the Works of Virgil Elizondo," *Worship* 65 (September 1991): 436-444.

_____"Liturgy, Popular Rites, and Popular Spirituality," *Worship* 63 (1989): 351-361. Reprinted in Spanish and English in *Liturgia y Canción* 3 (1991): 8-17.

_____"Marriage Celebrations in Mexican American Communities," *Liturgical Ministry,* 1996.

_____"Ministries and the Servant Community," With Roberto Piña and Yolanda Tarango. *Worship* 67 (1993): 351-360.

_____"Our Lady of Guadalupe Celebrations in San Antonio, Texas, 1840-41," *Journal of Hispano/Latino Theology* 1 (1993): 77-96.

_____"Tejano Lay Initiatives in Worship, 1830-1860." Working Paper Series, Cushwa Center for the Study of American Catholicism. University of Notre Dame, October 1993.

_____"U.S. Hispanic Catholics and Liturgical Reform," *America* 169 (1993): 18-19.

Pecharromán, Oridio. "Misa, Mesa y Musa." *Catholic Standard,* (September 24, 1970)

Pérez, Arturo, ed. *Así Es: Stories of Hispanic Spirituality.* Collegeville, MN: The Liturgical Press, 1994.

_____ *Novenario Por Los Difuntos.* Chicago: Liturgy Training Publications, 1987.

_____Finding & Forming Sponsors. "Hispanic Traditions of Padrinos & Madrinas." Chicago: Liturgy Training Publications, 1988.

_____ *Popular Catholicism: A Hispanic Perspective.* Washington, DC: Pastoral Press, 1988.

_____, and Mark Francis, *Primero Dios.* Chicago, IL: Liturgy Training Publications, 1997.

_____"Baptism in the Hispanic Community," *Emmanuel Magazine* 87 (1981): No. 2.

_____"Lent: Conversion Liturgy," *Hosanna* 1 (Spring 1983): No. 1.

_____"Recurso: Guadalupe," *Liturgy 80,* November and December, 1984).

_____"Novenario," *Liturgy 80* October, 1985.

_____"Novenario, Part II," *Liturgy 80* November and December, 1985.

_____"Worship in a Multicultural Community," *Liturgy 80,* May and June, 1986.

_____"Soñando -Multiculturally," *Liturgy 80* August and September, 1986.

_____"Joseph's Coat of Many Colors," *Liturgy 80* July, 1987.

_____"Signs of the Times: Towards a Hispanic Rite, Quizás," *New Theology Review* 3 (November 1990).

_____"The Fifth Century of Evangelization in the Americas," *Liturgy,* 9 (Fall 1991).

_____"History of Hispanic Liturgy from 1965." *Hispanic Catholic Culture in The U.S.: Issues and Concerns,* Notre Dame, IN: University of Notre Dame, 1994.

_____"Hispanic Spirituality," *The Modern Catholic Encyclopedia.* Collegeville: The Liturgical Press, 1994.

Ramírez, Ricardo. "Is the Prophet Speaking Spanish?" *Living Worship* (1977).

_____"Liturgy from the Mexican American Perspective," *Worship* 51 (July 1977).

_____"Environment in the Service of the Ambiente," *Liturgy* (1978).

_____ *Fiesta, Worship, and the Family: Essays on Mexican American Perception on Liturgy and Family Life.* San Antonio: MACC, 1981.

_____"Reflections on the Hispanization of the Liturgy," *Worship* 57 (1983).

_____"Hispanic Spirituality," _Social Thought_ 11 (Summer 1985).

_____ _El Descubrimiento del Tesoro más Rico en la Liturgia: El Rito de la Iniciación Cristiana para Adultos._ Miami: Instituto de Liturgia Hispana, 1986.

Sosa, Juan J. "La Santería." _Cuba: Diáspora,_ Christian Commitment Foundation, Inc., (1974): 66-78.

_____"Santa Bárbara y San Lázaro." _Cuba: Diáspora,_ Christian Commitment Foundation, Inc., (1976): 101-103.

_____"Religiosidad Popular." _Cuba: Diáspora,_ Christian Commitment Foundation, Inc., (1979): 27-29.

_____"An Anglo-Hispanic Dilemma: Liturgical Piety or Popular Piety" in Liturgy: Evangelization and Popular Devotions. _Liturgy: a Journal of the Liturgical Conference,_ 24:6 (November-December 1979): 7-9.

_____"Popular Piety: An Integral Element of the Conversion Process." _Christian Initiation Resources._ New York: Sadlier, 1980, vol.1: 249-254.

_____"El Ministerio de la Música Litúrgica en Nuestras Comunidades Hispanas," _Liturgy 80_ (October 1981): 10-11.

_____"Liturgy in Two Languages... Some Principles," _Pastoral Music._ (August-September 1981): vol. 5, 6:36-38.

_____"Illness and Healing in Hispanic Communities," in Liturgy: Ministries to the Sick. _Liturgy: A Journal of the Liturgical Conference,_ (1982): Vol. 2, 2:62-67.

_____"Let us Pray... en Español," in _Liturgy: A Journal of the Liturgical Conference,_ Spring, 1983: vol. 3, 2:63-67.

_____"Liturgy in Three Languages," _Pastoral Music_ February-March, 1983: 13-15.

_____"Religiosidad Popular y Sincretismo Religioso: Santería y Espiritismo." _Documentaciones Sureste._ Miami: Oficina Regional del Sureste para Asuntos Hispanos (Marzo, 1983): no. 4.

_____"Liturgia Hispana en Estados Unidos." _Notitiæ: Sacra Congregatio Pro Culto Divino._ Vatican City, October 1984, 20: 688-696.

_____"La Celebración," in _Speak the Truth in Love/Proclama la Verdad con Amor._ Washington, DC: Department of Education USCC, Catechetical Sunday September 21, 1986: 14-17.

_____ Criterios para las Celebraciones Litúrgicas en las Comunidades Hispanas. Miami: Instituto de Liturgia Hispana, Inc., 1988.

_____ "Texto Unico: A Unified Liturgical Text for Spanish-Speaking Catholics," *Liturgy 90*, May/June 1989: 9-10.

_____ "Los Símbolos Religiosos: Una Llamada a la Oración," *Phase*. Barcelona: Centre de Pastoral Litúrgica, año XXIX, no. 173 (1989), 403-410.

_____ "Renewal and Inculturation," in Liturgy: A Life to Share. *Liturgy: A Journal of the Liturgical Conference* (2) Winter 1990, 17-23.

_____ "Liturgy and Culture: Tradition and Creativity." *Worship and Ministry*. Orlando: Diocese of Orlando, 1991, 24-25.

_____ "The Fifth Centenary: A Historical Encounter with Prayer," *Liturgia y Canción* 1992, 8-10.

_____ "El V Centenario: Un Encuentro en la Oración," *Liturgia y Canción* 1992, 5-7.

_____ "Reflections from the Hispanic Viewpoint." in *The Awakening Church: Twenty-five years of Liturgical Renewal*. Lawrence J. Madden, S.J., ed. Collegeville: The Liturgical Press, 1992.

_____ "Liturgia, religiosidad popular y evangelización. El ejemplo de la liturgia hispana en Estados Unidos," *Phase*. Barcelona: Centre de Pastoral Litúrgica, año XXXII, no. 190 (1992), 295-301.

_____ "Hospitality for an by Musicians: Melody and Text," *Pastoral Music* February-March 1993, 18-21.

_____ Santa Bárbara y San Lázaro. Comité de Piedad Popular de la Arquidiócesis de Miami. Ministerio de Liturgia y Vida Espiritual, (bilingual publication/ publicación bilingüe), 1994.

_____ "The Rite of Marriage in Hispanic Communities," *Liturgia y Canción, 1996*.

Vela, Rudy. "Hispanic Bienvenida: An Embrace and a Kiss," *Pastoral Music* 13 (5) June-July 1989.

Vidal, Jaime. "Popular Religion in the Lands of Origin of New York's Hispanic Population." *Hispanics in New York: Religious, Cultural, and Social Experiences*, vol. 2 (NY: Office of Pastoral Research of the Archdiocese of New York, 1982).

_____ "Popular Religion Among Hispanics in the General Area of the Archdioceses of Newark," *Presencia Nueva: Knowledge for Service and Hope* (Newark, NJ: Office of Research & Planning, 1988).

Zelada, Rogelio. *Manual para Proclamadores de la Palabra: Comentarios Bíblicos*, Ciclo A. Chicago: Liturgy Training Publications, 1996.

_____ *Manual para Proclamadores de la Palabra: Comentarios Bíblicos*, Ciclo C. Chicago: Liturgy Training Publications, 1995.

_____ *Manual para Proclamadores de la Palabra: Comentarios Bíblicos*, Ciclo B. Chicago: Liturgy Training Publications, 1994.

_____ *Manual para Proclamadores de la Palabra: Comentarios Bíblicos*, Ciclo A. Chicago: Liturgy Training Publications, 1993.

_____ *Manual para Proclamadores de la Palabra: Comentarios Bíblicos*, Ciclo C. Chicago: Liturgy Training Publications, 1992.

_____ "Las Advocaciones Marianas en la Religiosidad Popular Latinoamericana." *Documentaciones Sureste*. Miami: S.E.P.I. Publications, 1996.

_____ *Inculturación*. S.E.P.I. Publications, Documentaciones Sureste. Miami: S.E.P.I. Publications, 1996.

_____ "La Biblia y su Uso Pastoral." *Video y Manual de uso*. Raleigh: Catholic Communications, Sepi/Diocese of Raleigh, 1992.

_____ "Para Vivir en Adviento" y "Representación Navideña," 2 artículos bilingües. *Liturgia y Canción*. Portland: Oregon Catholic Press, Noviembre-Febrero, 1992.

_____ "De las Cenizas a la Pascua: en Camino hacia el Misterio Pascual," y "Sugerencias para los Estandartes," 2 artículos bilingües. Portland: Oregon Catholic Press, Febrero-Mayo, 1991.

_____ , con Mons. A. Román. "Religiosidad Popular, las Imágenes de María en la Piedad Popular Latinoamericana." San Antonio: Instituto de Liturgia Hispana, 1990.

The *Instituto de Liturgia Hispana* has assisted the Bishops' Committee on the Liturgy (BCL) of the National Conference of Catholic Bishops of the United States (NCCB) in the preparation of Spanish translation of official texts, such as:

La música en el culto católico (Music in Catholic Worship/Liturgical Music Today, 1984)

La ambientación y el arte en el culto católico (Environment and Art in Catholic Worship, 1986)

Rito de la iniciación cristiana de adultos (Rite of Christian Initiation of Adults, 1991)

Sunday Celebrations in the Absence of a Priest (bilingual ed. 1994)

LITURGICAL MUSIC:

Several current and former members of the Instituto have published music for use in prayer and liturgy. Below is a list of some of these authors as well as their publishers:

Lorenzo Florián -World Library/J.S. Paluch; GIA Publications

María Pérez-Rudisill -Archdiocese of Miami -Office of Worship

Mary Frances Reza -Oregon Catholic Press

José Rubio -Oregon Catholic Press

Juan Sosa -Archdiocese of Miami -Office of Worship; Oregon Catholic Press

Damaris Thillet -World Library/J.S. Paluch

Rogelio Zelada -Archdiocese of Miami -Office of Worship.

PUBLICATIONS OF THE
INSTITUTO DE LITURGIA HISPANA

Amén -quarterly newsletter.

Religiosidad Popular: Las imágenes de Jesucristo y la Virgen María en América Latina (1990).

El Misterio de Fe -in conjunction with the FDLC, (The Mystery of Faith, rev. ed. 1991).

INSTITUTO DE LITURGIA HISPANA
P.O. BOX 29387
WASHINGTON, D.C. 20017-0387

125

Glossary

Sylvia Sánchez

Abuelo/a, Abuelito/a — "Grandfather / Grandmother." (-ito/-ita is a suffix indicating affection.)

Altarcito — "Little altar": a place of honor in a home reserved for the Lord, the Virgin, or the family's favored saint; also serves as a display area for photos of deceased loved ones.

Ahijado/a — Godson/Goddaughter

Arras — "Pledge": refers to something valuable given to signify that a contract has been agreed to, such as the coins that are exchanged between bride and groom during the wedding ceremony.

Capilla — "Chapel": a small building used for worship; or that part a church which contains the Blessed Sacrament.

Cruz de Mayo — Celebration in remembrance of the discovery of the Holy Cross (May 3 on the old liturgical calendar). In certain regions of Spain there are parades in which a priest goes through the crowd blessing crucifixes. The holy cross has replaced the *mayos*, or maypole-trees, that stood decorated in plazas and on sidewalks.

Chambelán — "Gentleman": the boys who form the retinue of a *Quinceañera* (festival of the fifteenth birthday).

Cojín — The small pillow for the rings that will be exchanged by bride and groom.

Compadre/Comadre — Relationship between the godfather/godmother and the parents of the godchildren.

Consideraciones del Rosario, las — In certain parts of Mexico, the term used for the mysteries of the rosary.

Dama — "Lady": one of the girls forming the retinue of a *Quinceañera* (festival of the fifteenth birthday).

Depósito — The reserved eucharist.

Diablo/Diablito—"Devil/little devil": in the dance of the *matachines*, the person who goes around making fun of others.

Día de los Muertos — All Souls Day, November 2. In some places it is customary for people to pray and eat in the cemetery next to the graves of their loved ones.

Encuentro, el Santo — Refers to the moment when Jesus "encounters" his mother on the road to Calvary and also to their imagined meeting after Jesus rose from the dead. In some cities these "encounters" are celebrated in public ceremonies on Good Friday and Easter Sunday.

Espiritismo — A superstition that attempts to call forth and reveal the spirits of the dead.

Fiestas — "Feast, celebration": any solemn commemoration of an important event, whether religious or secular.

Guadalupe, Nuestra Señora de — Title given to the Virgin Mary on the occasion of her appearance in the hills of Tepeyac, Mexico (1531). The Patron of Mexico and Queen of the Americas.

Inculturación — The process of learning and assimilating cultural values through experience and instruction. The term also is being used to refer to the expression of gospel values within a particular culture. Christian message of cultural evangelization.

Lazo — A "rope" with an artistic knot, which is symbolic of the marital union.

Mampucho — A grotesque figure, a rag doll or a puppet; in slang, an intrusive person.

Mañanitas, las — "Little morning song": a piece of music, typical of Mexico, that is used to greet and/or honor a person very early in the morning of his or her birthday.

Matachines — The performers of a ritual dance of pre-Hispanic origin. This tradition continues in northern and some parts of central Mexico, as well as in sections of the southeastern United States. The ritual dancers usually perform for the Virgin of Guadalupe.

Mestizo (Mestizaje) — The intermarriage of Europeans and Native Americans. Also, any offspring of racially distinct parents.

Miércoles de Ceniza — Ash Wednesday, the first day of the Lenten season.

Mística — That part of theology that deals with spirituality. Also, a very intimate union with God achieved by way of meditation and prayer.

Monumento — "Monument": a small sepulchre, tomb, or mausoleum, usually for the preservation of a relic. Also, the altar constructed on Holy Thursday to store the consecrated hosts that are shared in communion on Good Friday.

Mujerista — (see *teología mujerista o feminista*)

Nacimiento — "Birth." Also, the depiction of a manger scene.

Novenarios — A period of nine days dedicated to praying for someone or something specific. Also, the prayers, masses, and rosaries offered during the nine days following a person's death.

Padrino/Madrina — "Little father/mother": the sponsors that present and accompany another person during a sacrament or a rite of passage (baptism, confirmation, marriage, fifteenth birthday, etc.) and who promise to support them throughout their lives.

Pastoral de Conjunto — The different ministries of the Church that work independently but in harmony with each other. A key feature of the *Pastoral* is a spirit of collaboration between laity and clergy.

Pastorela — "Shepherd's play" featuring dancing, singing, and poetry that celebrates the birth of Christ. In most versions of the play, the devil tries to stop the shepherds from reaching Bethlehem.

Peregrinación — "Pilgrimage": a trip made to a religious shrine, usually to offer respect and admiration for the place one is visiting.

Pésame — "Condolence, sympathy": the display of grief for one who has died.

Piñata — A decorated earthenware container, originally made in the form of a seven-pointed star, which is filled with sweets and then hung from the roof. Participants try to break the container open by swinging a stick at it while blindfolded. The custom was begun by missionaries at the time of the conquistadors in Mexico.

Religiosidad Popular — The manifestation of a people's religious faith and devotion through culture, specific rites and rituals.

Posa, la — Tolling of the bells to announce the death of a member of the community (see *Toques para los muertos*). Also, a small enclosure where the priest stands to intone the prayer for the dead.

Posada — "Inn" or "hostel": the tradition of *las posadas* refers to the re-enactment over a period of nine days of Mary and Joseph's search for shelter in Bethlehem. On the ninth day (Christmas Eve), they find shelter and the baby Jesus is born.

Presentacion del Niño, la — The custom of presenting a newborn child to the church community to give thanks and to ask for God's blessing, modeled after the presentation of the baby Jesus in chapter 2 of Luke's gospel.

Pueblo — The "people" who comprise a nation, region, or place. The *pueblo de Dios* are the people who have been called together and united by God.

Quince Años/Quinceañera — The celebration of a child's fifteenth birthday. *La Quinceañera* is also a term used for the girl (or boy: *-ro*) who turns fifteen years of age.

Rezanderos/-as — Refers to those people within a community that are called to pray with community groups, usually in homes, for someone or something specific. In rural areas and communities, the *rezanderos/-as* are typically women.

Rito Mozarabe — A distinct rite of the Catholic Church established during the Arab occupation of Spain; this rite is still celebrated in parts of Toledo and Salamanca.

Santería — A cult rising out of superstitions regarding the saints. Also, the art of sculpting images of the saints.

Santísimo, el — The Blessed Sacrament

Siete Palabras, las — The "seven final words" uttered by Christ on the cross. Also, the act of meditating on these words during the noon service on Good Friday.

Tarascas — Monstrous figures simulating dragons that are used in parades on *Corpus Christi*.

Teología Mujerista o Feminista — A feminine approach to theology. The expression originated in the United States, through the efforts of a distinguished group of Hispanic women theologians.

Toques para los Muertos, los — The tolling of the church bells to announce the death of a member of the community.

Tres Reyes Magos, los — The three Magi or Kings who came to see the newborn Jesus. In Hispanic countries, gifts are given to children on Epiphany in remembrance of the gifts of the *tres reyes*.

Vals — "Waltz": a quick, elegant dance (measured in three beats) traditionally performed during a *Quinceañera*.

Vela — "Candle." Also, "vigil," such as the time keeping watch before the blessed sacrament, or the time one spends near a deceased loved one during a wake. *La vela* can also refer to the act of covering the bride and groom with a *velo* (veil) during a marriage ceremony.

Vía Crucis, el Santo —The "way of the cross": a devotion dating to the 18th century that consists of following Jesus' path to his death and burial at fourteen stations.

Vigilia — "Vigil": the evening and night before an important festival or celebration.

Visitación, la — "Visitation": commemorates the visit of Mary to her cousin Elizabeth before the birth of John the Baptist.